A Survey of Family Literacy

in the United States

LESLEY MANDEL MORROW
Rutgers University, New Brunswick, New Jersey

DIANE H. TRACEY
Kean College, Union, New Jersey

CATERINA MARCONE MAXWELL
Rutgers University, New Brunswick, New Jersey

EDITORS

INTERNATIONAL READING ASSOCIATION
NEWARK, DELAWARE 19714, USA

The International Reading Association attempts, through its publications,
to provide a forum for a wide spectrum of opinions on reading. This policy permits divergent viewpoints without assuming the endorsement of the
Association.

Director of Publications   Joan M. Irwin
Associate Editor   Christian A. Kempers
Assistant Editor   Amy L. Trefsger Miles
Editorial Assistant   Janet Parrack
Production Department Manager   Iona Sauscermen
Graphic Design Coordinator   Boni Nash
Design Consultant   Larry Husfelt
Desktop Publishing Supervisor   Wendy Mazur
Desktop Publishing   Anette Schütz-Ruff
                       Cheryl Strum
Proofing   David Roberts

Library of Congress Cataloging in Publication Data
    A survey of family literacy in the United States/Lesley Mandel Morrow,
Diane H. Tracey, Caterina Marcone Maxwell, editors
        p.   cm.
    Includes bibliographical references and index.
    1. Family literacy programs—United States—Directories.   2. Literacy—
Social aspects—United States.   3. Reading—Parent participation—United
States.   I. Morrow, Lesley Mandel.   II. Tracey, Diane H.   III. Maxwell,
Caterina Marcone.   IV. International Reading Association.
LC151.S87   1995   92-5525
302.2'44—dc20   CIP
ISBN 0-87207-131-6 (softcover)

Photo credits: Laima Druskis, p. 1.; Boston University Photo Services, p. 49;
Lou Coopey, p. 87; Rick Reinhard (©Reading Is Fundamental, Inc. Used with
permission), p. 111.

Dedication

THIS BOOK IS DEDICATED TO OUR FAMILIES:

FRANK AND STEPHANIE

STEPHEN, JULIA, AND KATHERINE

BRUCE AND IAN

IT IS ALSO DEDICATED TO THE FAMILIES OF THE IRA FAMILY LITERACY COMMISSION AND THE FAMILIES OF THE INTERNATIONAL READING ASSOCIATION.

Acknowledgment

THE PREPARATION OF THIS MONOGRAPH INCLUDED THE HELP OF MANY PEOPLE. WE WOULD LIKE TO THANK BETTY WELT FOR THE RESEARCH SHE DID IN COLLECTING INFORMATION ON AGENCIES AND ASSOCIATIONS THAT DEAL WITH FAMILY LITERACY AND AMY BUSCH, WHO HELPED TO COLLECT MANY OF THE ANNOTATIONS IN-CLUDED IN THIS VOLUME. IN ADDITION, THANK YOU TO THE MANY OTHER RUTGERS UNIVERSITY STUDENTS WHO WORKED ON COMPUTER SEARCHES TO COLLECT PRO-GRAMS TO SELECT FOR ANNOTATIONS.

Contents

Introduction

AWARENESS ABOUT THE POWERFUL INFLUENCE OF THE FAMILY ON CHILDREN'S LITERACY DEVELOPMENT HAS GAINED NATIONAL PROMINENCE IN RECENT YEARS. INCREASINGLY, EDUCATORS, PARENTS, POLICY MAKERS, AND CITIZENS FROM ALL WALKS OF LIFE ARE BEING TOLD ABOUT THE IMPORTANCE OF PARENTS READING TO THEIR CHILDREN AT HOME. WE HAVE ALSO BEEN TOLD ABOUT THE CRITICAL NATURE OF LITERACY EXPERIENCES AT HOME AND ABOUT THE VALUE OF PARENTAL INVOLVEMENT IN CHILDREN'S SCHOOL EXPERIENCES FROM EARLY CHILDHOOD THROUGH ADOLESCENCE. THE INTEREST IN AND SUPPORT OF HOW LITERACY IS USED IN FAMILIES, AS WELL AS THE STUDY OF THE RELATIONSHIP BETWEEN THE USE OF LITERACY IN FAMILIES AND THE ACADEMIC ACHIEVEMENT OF THOSE CHILDREN, ALONG WITH THE DESIGN, IMPLEMENTATION, AND EVALUATION OF PROGRAMS TO FACILITATE LITERACY DEVELOPMENT IN FAMILIES HAVE ALL BECOME SYNONYMOUS WITH THE TERM "FAMILY LITERACY." HOWEVER, WHILE THE TERM FAMILY LITERACY IS FAMILIAR TO MANY, IT IS CLEARLY UNDERSTOOD BY FEW.

This volume attempts to help educators, parents, and policy makers understand the concept of family literacy by (1) explaining the definition, brief historical development, and overview of the current state of family literacy in the United States, (2) disseminating information regarding types of family literacy initiatives currently underway in this country, and (3) acting as a resource guide for those interested in obtaining specific information about particular family literacy programs in the United States. This information will be of interest both to individuals new to the study of family literacy and those who are already familiar with the field.

The Definition of Family Literacy

The definition of family literacy, like the definition of literacy itself, is a debatable construct. In a recent article supported by International Reading Association's Family Literacy Commission (Morrow & Paratore, 1993), it was noted that even among professionals within the field, differing perspectives regarding the scope and depth of the issue and its definition are held. The commission, instead of citing an exact definition, determined that their perspective of family literacy would reflect the broadest possible orientation to the topic. As such, the commission recommended that family literacy be considered a complex concept, associated with many different beliefs about the relationships between families and literacy. Among these beliefs are that family literacy is composed of both mainstream and non-mainstream families, that literacy extends beyond "school-based" activities into the daily, functional use of literacy by families, that family literacy activities reflect the ethnic, racial, and cultural heritages of families, and that family literacy efforts can be initiated by organizations outside of the families. Although the absence of a concise definition of family literacy may, at first, be slightly uncomfortable for those new to the field, many within the field believe that the richness gained from holding a broad perspective about family literacy far outweighs the benefits of a precise but narrow understanding of the topic (Auerbach, 1989; Taylor, 1983). Thus, the position held by the writers of this book is that family literacy refers to a complex concept associated with many different beliefs about the relationships between families and the development of literacy.

The Beginning of Family Literacy in the United States

Studies relating to the influence of "the family as educator" had their earliest roots in the work of anthropologists and sociologists who studied the general concept of the family. Leichter (1974) states that anthropologists and sociologists have traditionally held very broad understandings of the relationships between families and education. For example, she observes that anthropological and sociological studies have examined families in both non-literate and highly industrialized societies, that the purposes of the studies have ranged from those interested in the social organization of the family to those interested in therapeutic interventions, and that the definitions of the concept of a family have included both nuclear and extended family units. Leichter states that, in contrast to anthropologists and sociologists, educators have traditionally held a much narrower view of the relationships between families and education, such as an emphasis solely on nuclear families within industrialized societies, a deficit orientation to the educational problems of the poor and disadvantaged, and cognitive orientation to the effects of parental behavior on children's academic achievement accompanied by "a striking concern with outcomes" (Leichter, 1974, p. 10).

Hundreds of studies have documented the relationships within "families as educators," but the majority of these investigations have been rooted in either anthropologic/sociologic or educational orientations to the topic. Each of these fields then gave rise to specific lines of research inquiries which ultimately led to an awareness of the striking role of families in children's literacy development. Examples of lines of research within education that have led to this realization include studies of the influence of parents on children's oral language development (Bernstein, 1970; Brown, 1973; Brown & Bellugi, 1964; Snow, 1977; 1983), studies of parents' book reading habits with young children (Altwerger, Diesel-Faxon, & Dockstader-Anderson, 1985; Flood, 1977; Ninio & Bruner, 1978; Roser & Martinez, 1985; Snow, 1983; Teale, 1981), studies of early readers (Clark, 1976; Durkin, 1966; Radecki, 1987), and studies of parental involvement on the academic achievement of school-age children (Bempechat, 1990; Caplan, Choy, & Whitmore, 1992). Each of these lines of research, as well as lines of research from the fields of anthropology and sociology, has contributed to our present day understanding of the role of families in children's literacy development.

The Current State of Family Literacy in the United States

The increase in public awareness about the role of the family in children's literacy development underscores the growing prominence of family literacy in our culture. The current state of family literacy may be best understood by examining the initiatives that are presently underway at federal, state, and local levels and by highlighting the most pressing issues now facing the field.

Federal Initiatives

According to Nickse (1993), federal legislation is the primary source of support for family literacy programs in this country. She lists the many acts and titles that presently support the family literacy movement: The Adult Education Act (Titles II and III), The Library and Construction Act (Titles I and VI), The Head Start Act, The Family Support Act of 1988 (Title IV-A), and several programs in the Elementary and Secondary Education Act, including Chapter 1, Even Start, Title VII Bilingual Education, and Title III, Part B the Family School Partnership Program. Of these, Even Start was the first federally funded initiative to be entirely devoted to family literacy. Signed into law by President Reagan in 1988, Even Start stipulated that funded programs needed to offer a combination of adult basic education, parenting education, and early childhood education information to its participants. Since 1988, $70 million dollars in federal funds have helped hundreds of family literacy programs across the United States (Brizius & Foster, 1993). At present, evaluation of Even Start is the largest family literacy evaluation project ever undertaken in this country (see Program Evaluation below).

The National Center for Family Literacy (NCFL) in Louisville, Kentucky, is an organization designed to disseminate information about family literacy and facilitate the implementation of family literacy programs throughout the country. This organization trains educators and policy makers to design, implement, and evaluate family literacy programs using a specific model of training, the Kenan Model. This model advocates that family literacy programs should have four components: (1) parent literacy education, (2) early childhood education, (3) support groups for parents, and (4) opportunities for planned interactions between parents and children. Since its establishment in 1989, NCFL has trained support staff for over 900 family literacy programs throughout the United States and has sponsored annual National Family Literacy Conferences.

Two other organizations, Reading is Fundamental (RIF) and The Barbara Bush Foundation for Family Literacy, have been notably instrumental in promoting family literacy initiatives at the national level. RIF is a national nonprofit organization in Washington D.C., that was formed in 1966 to promote children's reading. Supported by corporate sponsors, foundation grants, and federal line budgeting, the organization originally provided assistance to local groups in obtaining and distributing books for children at low cost and by creating motivational activities and events to support children's reading. While the organization still maintains these original functions, since 1982 it has also developed programs that guide and support parents in their roles as their children's first teachers and has published a guide to its own family literacy programs (Reading Is Fundamental, 1991). Many of the programs described in this volume are associated with the RIF initiative.

Like RIF, The Barbara Bush Foundation is also a nationally recognized program that has brought a great amount of attention to the issue of family literacy in the United States. The foundation has published a book describing 10 model family literacy programs in the country (The Barbara Bush Foundation for Family Literacy, 1989) and also offers grants annually to support existing family initiatives. Other recent efforts currently underway to extend the family literacy movement at the national level include attempting to incorporate a family literacy component into Head Start programs and into President Clinton's Welfare Reform package. According to Andrew Hartman, the newly appointed director of the National Institute for Literacy, "the future for family literacy at the federal policy level looks bright" (Hartman, 1994, p. 2).

State Initiatives

While family literacy has enjoyed wide success at the federal level, state governments have been slower to financially support these initiatives (Brizius & Foster, 1993). It has been suggested that this hesitancy stems not from a lack of philosophical support regarding the importance or effectiveness of family literacy programs, but from a lack of financial resources available for such endeavors (Brizius & Foster, 1993). For example, in a report about meeting the educational needs of the 21st century, the New Jersey Council on Adult Education and Literacy demonstrated its commitment to the concept of family literacy by concluding that family literacy and promoting the concept of the family as educator were central to meeting the future literacy needs of New Jersey communities (New Jersey State Council on Adult Education, 1993). Similarly, the Nevada Literacy 2000 report, the first statewide master plan for Nevada literacy, cited family literacy as a major component in its educational plans for the future (Literacy Coalition Advisory Council, 1993). Thus, while state governments have not, for the most part, had the financial resources to independently back family literacy initiatives in the past, many now appear to be planning to incorporate family literacy into their future plans. The states of Hawaii and Kentucky, which currently do possess state funded family literacy programs, are pioneers in this area. Many believe that the future involvement of state government in the family literacy movement will arise from shifts in the administration of the Even Start program. It is expected that administration of the program will move from the federal government, which presently administers it, to administration by individual state governments (Nickse, 1993).

Local Initiatives

There has been much activity related to family literacy at the local level as well as at the national and state levels. Visible trends at the local levels include: (1) an emphasis on collaboration between local level agencies, (2) the development of centralized services for families, and (3) the emergence of family literacy grass-roots initiatives.

With regard to the first trend, it has been stated that the drive toward the development of partnerships between local level organizations is one of the cornerstones of the family literacy movement (Gaber, 1993). This emphasis on collaboration and partnerships has grown largely as a by-product of agencies with similar goals realizing the financial savings and potential for increased effectiveness associated with collaborative efforts. Collaboration and partnerships between different groups such as universities, public schools, early childhood education programs, adult literacy programs, and businesses have been advocated as one of the most promising avenues for continued growth of the family literacy movement (Brizius & Foster, 1993; Gaber, 1993).

The trend toward the centralization of services for families is closely related to the notion of collaboration described above. The concept of centralization of services suggests that families are best served when all related support is available through a "single point of entry" system (Betancourt, 1995, p. 6). Such a system is based on a "family-centered model" that "uses family needs and desires to guide all aspects of service delivery and seeks to strengthen the family's ability to meet their own needs (Betancourt, 1995, p. 9). In such a model, family literacy needs and programs fall under the wider umbrella of general family support services. The states of Rhode Island and California have already begun implementing centralized family social services programs that include family literacy components.

The development of grassroots family literacy movements is a third trend currently visible at the local level. In this situation, described by Brizius and Foster (1993) as the fastest growing component of the family literacy movement, individuals from differing sectors of a community take it upon themselves to initiate a family literacy project in their hometown or city. Frequently, national level organizations such as RIF are then contacted for guidelines to develop, implement, administer, and evaluate the local programs. Help for individuals interested in starting a grassroots family literacy program in their community is beginning to become available through books, newsletters, videos, conferences, and professional training programs; however, the interest and desire for information on this topic appears to be greater than the current volume of information that is easily accessible to the general public.

Program Evaluation

As funding for family literacy programs at the national, state, and local levels increases to unprecedented levels, family literacy professionals are, justifiably, being asked to document the effectiveness of their programs and projects. The evaluation of family literacy initiatives, however, is an aspect of the field which is still in its infancy (Brizius & Foster, 1993). As such, issues regarding what should be measured and how it should be measured are presently under careful scrutiny and debate.

In one attempt to address the issue of the evaluation of family literacy programs Nickse (1993) has applied a general program evaluation framework developed by Jacobs (1988) to the specific field of family literacy. The framework presents five developmental levels of program evaluation, each more detailed and complex than the previous one. The first level focuses on pre-implementation concerns such as defining the problem and assessing the need for services. The second level focuses on accountability and tries to assess the population being served and the services being provided. The third level of the framework focuses on the issue of clarification, such as how the client can be better served. The fourth level of the framework addresses the issue of measurement of short-term objectives, and the fifth level uses experimental research to evaluate long-term effects of program participation. According to Nickse (1993) the application of a framework such as this to family literacy programming is a useful beginning point for evaluation.

To date, the evaluation of the federally funded Even Start program is the most comprehensive family literacy evaluation thus far undertaken in this country. A brief summary of the evaluation is reported here to provide readers with an example of how high quality evaluation of family programs can be completed as well as to share information regarding the reported effectiveness of this program. The report used an experimental design and qualitative research methods to comprehensively assess the effectiveness of Even Start's three core program elements: parenting education, early childhood education, and adult literacy education. Results indicated that Even Start has been extremely effective in providing services to its target population. Participation in adult education programs rose from approximately 35% to 90%; participation in parenting education rose from approximately 8% to 93%; and participation in early childhood education programming rose from approximately 60% to 98%. With respect to the effects of program participation, significant improvement for children in Even Start (versus control group children) was found on a formal test of preschool abilities, the Preschool Inventory. Improvement on the Peabody Picture Vocabulary Test was also found, but significant differences were not found between the Even Start and control group children. Significant differences between the Even Start and control group children on a test developed for the project, the

Emergent Literacy Test, also were not found. With respect to parental literacy, Even Start parents were significantly more likely than controls to obtain a high school General Equivalency Diploma; however, no measurable program effects were detectable on a survey evaluating reading and writing activities in the home. Improvement of functional literacy rates for the Even Start adults was found to correlate with the amount of actual program attendance. The study of the effects of the Even Start program on parenting abilities showed significant improvement for the Even Start parents (versus controls) in the areas of providing reading materials in the home, and in parental expectations regarding the likelihood that their children would graduate from high school. Program effects were not found for frequency of depressive symptoms, measurement of locus of control, and performance on a parent-child reading task. Finally, minimal overall effects on family functioning were reported as measured by adult perceived social support, adequacy of financial resources, income levels, and employment status. However, according to the authors, these factors were measured only for a single-year period and were not expected to be affected given the relatively short time period during which they were assessed. Readers interested in a more comprehensive understanding of the evaluation of the Even Start program are urged to read the original evaluation report (St. Pierre, Swartz, Murray, Deck, & Nickel, 1993).

In sum, although the evaluation of Even Start demonstrates that high quality assessment of family literacy programs is possible, most programs have only minimal, if any, program evaluation in place. Nickse (1993) suggests that sufficient resources to fund evaluation projects as well as training for family literacy professionals are needed to strengthen this dimension of family literacy service. In short, the evaluation of family literacy programs is an aspect of the field which must mature if the future of the family literacy movement is to be safeguarded. It is presently one of the most pressing concerns of the field facing policy makers and practitioners.

Philosophical Issues Within the Family Literacy Movement

No discussion of the current state of family literacy is complete without mention of the philosophical concerns underlining the field. Specifically, great concern has been voiced by some writers regarding the use of the deficit hypothesis, or deficit model, in the field of family literacy (Auerbach, 1989; Delgado-Gaitan, 1992; Taylor, 1993, 1994). Auerbach (1989) brought this issue to the educational community's attention in an article that criticized family literacy programs that sought to teach immigrant and refugee parents to do traditional school-like activities in the home via the "transmission model," a model in which information is transmitted in one direction: from the school to the parents and then to the child. Auerbach argued that the transmission model makes many false assumptions which, in turn, lead to a deficit model belief system:

> The first assumption is that language-minority students come from literacy-impoverished homes where education is not valued or supported. The second assumption is that family literacy involves a one-way transfer of skills from parents to children. Third, this model assumes that success is determined by the parents' ability to support and extend school-like activities in the home. The fourth assumption is that school practices are adequate and that it is home factors that will determine who succeeds. And fifth, the model assumes that parents' own problems get in the way of creating positive family literacy contexts.

> Taken together, these assumptions contribute to a new version of the deficit hypothesis, placing the locus of responsibility for literacy problems with the family. The danger is that, left unexamined, these assumptions will justify a model that blames the victim by attributing literacy problems largely to family inadequacies.

> (Auerbach, 1989, p. 169)

Furthermore, Auerbach (1989), Taylor (1993, 1994), and Taylor and Dorsey-Gaines (1988) "argue that it is the lack of social, political, and economic support for parents...(in dealing with society) that puts their children at risk," rather than parents' lack of support for their children's literacy development (Auerbach, 1989, p. 175). Indeed, it has been shown repeatedly that parents from poor, minority, and immigrant families highly value and strongly support their children's literacy development (Chall & Snow, 1982; Delgado-Gaitan, 1992; Taylor & Dorsey-Gaines, 1988). Shanahan (1994) has extended the concerns voiced by deficit model critics by questioning educators' moral right to instill white, middle-class values and patterns of interaction in families from culturally and ethnically diverse communities.

Writers and researchers opposing the deficit model propose viewpoints being referred to as the *wealth model**. This model stresses that all families have strengths and have intact literacy patterns within the home. Proponents of the wealth model emphasize that family literacy providers need to find out which literacy patterns exist within families and build on those patterns, rather than imposing traditional, mainstream school-like activities on parents. In addition, family literacy providers need to find out what types of literacy interactions are culturally consistent with family functioning. In contrast to being based on the transmission model, which is a school driven curriculum, the wealth model suggests that the family literacy curriculum be based on the needs voiced by the family literacy clients. Auerbach (1989) writes, "In this alternative formulation, housing, education, work, and health issues are acknowledged and explored in the classroom, with literacy becoming a tool for addressing these issues, and cultural differences are perceived as strengths and resources that can bridge the gap between home and school" (p. 176).

Overview

This book aims to address the pressing need for more information about the topic of family literacy in general and about specific programs in particular that have been observed by professionals working within the field, as well as by the Family Literacy Commission of the International Reading Association, a group appointed to study issues related to family literature and disseminate information about programs and concerns. The book is divided into five sections. The following section provides annotations of parent involvement programs, which are designed to work with parents for the primary purpose of improving their children's literacy development. These programs cover a wide spectrum of age groups and populations and originate from a variety of organizations including schools, libraries, and community services groups. Often these programs are collaborative efforts supported by several social service groups. The third section of the book provides annotations of intergenerational family literacy programs. The primary focus of intergenerational programs is the literacy achievement of both parents and their children. Thus, in intergenerational programs both adults and children attend classes to facilitate their own literacy progress. Also, the adults may attend parenting classes or vocational training while the children participate in high quality educational programs. The fourth section of the book provides abstracts of research on naturally occurring literacy within the field of family literacy. These projects study the ways in which families naturally use literacy during the routines of their daily lives. Often this research does not have a deliberate connection with the school curriculum but, rather, informs educators about families' natural use of literacy practices. The fifth section of the book provides a resource of agencies and associations currently active within the field of family literacy, while the sixth section of the book provides references for further reading about family literacy. These organizations and references will have further information about family literacy for the interested reader. It is the intent of the authors that this volume contribute to the continued growth of the family literacy movement throughout this country and beyond by providing information about family literacy programs, research efforts, and support organizations that presently exist within the field.

*Since the purpose of this volume is to present initiatives that exist in the United States, all viewpoints have been represented in the annotations of programs.

References

Altwerger, B., Diehl-Faxon, J., & Dockstader-Anderson, K. (1985). Read-aloud events as meaning construction. *Language Arts, 62* (5), 476–484.

Auerbach, E.R. (1989). Toward a social-contextual approach to family literacy. *Harvard Educational Review, 59* (2), 165–181.

Bempechat, J. (1990). *The role of parent involvement in children's academic achievement: A review of the literature.* New York: ERIC Clearinghouse on Urban Education.

Bernstein, B. (1970). A sociolinguistic approach to socialization with some references to educability. In F. Williams (Ed.), *Language and poverty* (pp. 25–50). Chicago, IL: Markham.

Betancourt, J. (May, 1995). *Family program concept paper, Community education series, Children's Television Workshop.* Unpublished Manuscript.

Brizius, J.A., & Foster, S.A. (1993). *Generation to generation: Realizing the promise of family literacy.* Ypsilanti, MI: High/Scope.

Brown, R. (1973). *A first language: The early stages.* Cambridge, MA: Harvard University Press.

Brown, R., & Bellugi, U. (1964). Three processes in the child's acquistion of syntax. *Harvard Educational Review, 34,* 133–151.

The Barbara Bush Foundation for Family Literacy. (1989). *First teachers: A family literacy handbook for parents, policy-makers, and literacy providers.* Washington, DC: Author.Caplan, N., Choy, M.H., & Whitmore, J.K. (1992, February). Indochinese refugee families and academic achievement. *Scientific American,* 36–42.

Chall, J.S., & Snow, C. (1982). *Families and literacy: The contributions of out of school experiences to children's acquisition of literacy* (A final report to the National Institute of Education). Washington, DC: Authors.

Clark, M.M. (1976). *Young fluent readers.* London: Heinemann Educational Books.

Delgado-Gaitan, C. (1992). School matters in the Mexican-American home: Socializing children to education. *American Educational Research Journal, 29* (3), 495–513.

Durkin, D. (1966). *Children who read early.* New York: Teachers College Press.

Flood, J. (1977). Parental styles in reading episodes with young children. *The Reading Teacher, 30* (8), 864–867.

Gaber, D. (1993, April). Community based adult literacy programs: A vehicle for developing family literacy. In L. Morrow & J. Paratore (Chairs), *Family literacy and learning in schools: Building key partnerships.* Institute conducted at the Annual Convention of the International Reading Association, San Antonio, TX.

Hartman, A. (1993, December). Family literacy's link to federal policy. *National Center for Family Literacy, 5* (4), 1–2.

Jacobs, F. (1988). The five-tiered approach to evaluation: Context and implementation. In H. Weiss, & F. Jacobs (Eds.), *Evaluating family programs.* Hawthorne, NY: Aldine de Gruyter.

Leichter, H. (1974). *The family as educator.* New York: Teachers College Press.

Literacy Coalition Advisory Council. (1993). *Nevada Literacy 2000.* (ERIC Document Reproduction Service No. ED 361 528)

Morrow, L.M., & Paratore, J. (1993). Family literacy: Perspective and practices. *The Reading Teacher. 47* (3), 194–200.

New Jersey Council on Adult Education. (1993, October). *Adult literacy in New Jersey: Meeting the challenge of the 21st century.* (ERIC Document Reproduction Service No. ED 364 717)

Nickse, R. (1993). *A typology of family and intergenerational literacy programs: Implications for evaluation.* (ERIC Document Reproduction Service No. ED 362 766)

Ninio, A., & Bruner, J. (1978). The achievement and antecedents of labeling. *Journal of Child Language, 5*, 1–15.

Radecki, K.K. (1987). *An annotated bibliography of the literature examining the importance of adults reading aloud to children.* Washington, DC: U.S. Department of Education. (ERIC Document Reproduction Service No. ED 294 274)

Reading Is Fundamental, Inc. (1991). *A guide to RIF's family literacy programs.* Washington, DC: Author.

Roser, N., & Martinez, M. (1985). Roles adults play in preschoolers' response to literature. *Language Arts, 62* (5), 485–490.

Shanahan, T. (1994, May). *Family literacy: Exciting innovation or just another way to blame the victim?* Paper presented at the meeting of the International Reading Association, Toronto, Ontario.

Snow, C.E. (1977). Mothers' speech research: From input to interaction. In C.E. Snow & C.A. Ferguson (Eds.), *Talking to children: Language input and acquistion,* (pp. 31–49). New York: Cambridge University Press.

Snow, C.E. (1983). Literacy and language: Relationships during the preschool years. *Harvard Educational Review, 53* (2), 165–189.

St. Pierre, R., Swartz, J., Murray, S., Deck, D., & Nickel, P. (1993, October). *National evaluation of the Even Start Family Literacy Program.* (ERIC Document Reproduction Service No. ED 365 476)

Taylor, D. (1983). *Family Literacy.* Portsmouth, NH: Heinemann.

Taylor, D. (1993, April). *Family literacy: Special contexts within the community for children learning to read and write.* Paper presented at the meeting of the International Reading Association, San Antonio, TX.

Taylor, D. (1994, May). *The ideologies and ethics of family literacy pedagogies: A postformal perspective.* Paper presented at the meeting of the International Reading Association, Toronto, Ontario.

Taylor, D., & Dorsey-Gaines, C. (1988). *Growing up literate: Learning from inner-city families.* Portsmouth, NH: Heinemann.

Teale, W.H. (1981). Parents reading to their children: What we know and need to know. *Language Arts, 58* (8), 902–912.

Introduction

Parent Involvement Programs

PARENT INVOLVEMENT PROGRAMS ARE DE-
SIGNED TO WORK WITH PARENTS FOR THE PRIMARY PUR-
POSE OF IMPROVING THEIR CHILDREN'S LITERACY DEVEL-
OPMENT. THESE PROGRAMS COVER A WIDE SPECTRUM
OF AGE GROUPS AND POPULATIONS AND ORIGINATE
FROM A VARIETY OF ORGANIZATIONS INCLUDING
SCHOOLS, LIBRARIES, AND COMMUNITY SERVICES GROUPS.
OFTEN THESE PROGRAMS ARE COLLABORATIVE EFFORTS
SUPPORTED BY SEVERAL SOCIAL SERVICE AGENCIES.

Arkansas Home Instruction Program for
Preschool Youngsters (HIPPY)
Little Rock, Arkansas

Program Description ❖ The Home Instruction Program was developed in 1969 in Jerusalem by a team of educators at the Hebrew University to prepare immigrant children to enter the highly competitive Israeli education system. In 1985, Hillary Rodham Clinton, then first lady of Arkansas, decided to explore the possibility of bringing the program to the United States. The first HIPPY pilot program began in Little Rock, Arkansas, in 1986. As of 1988, there were 14 HIPPY sites in 23 Arkansas counties.

HIPPY is a home-based program that helps parents of preschoolers to prepare their children for success upon entering school. The programs are run through community centers, public school districts, YMCAs, community action agencies, and state educational cooperatives. Twice a month, a paraprofessional, who must be a parent from the same community, visits the parent in the program and works with him or her on biweekly lessons. Each paraprofessional works with 10 to 15 families, and each program has one coordinator for every 12 paraprofessionals. The instructional program is made up of packets of programmed materials that focus on language, problem solving, and discrimination skills. The packets increase in difficulty over a two-year period.

Storybooks are given to the families and are used to carry out language instruction. Parents are taught how to ask questions about details of vocabulary, content, and other story concepts. Daily worksheets are used to track lessons from the stories. The worksheets offer visual, tactile, and auditory exercises. Problem-solving exercises teach the children to sort, list, match, and group attributes. Parents are required to work with their children for at least 15 minutes a day, 5 days a week, 30 weeks annually for 2 years, the second half of which the child is in kindergarten. The mothers and fathers gather on alternating weeks for group meetings with their paraprofessionals and to share experiences and ideas with other parents.

Program Success ❖ Tests that were administered to children and parents before and after the program show evidence of significant gain. In the fall of 1986, only 6 percent of the children in one district who were about to enter HIPPY received average scores on testing, and none were above average. In the spring of 1988, the second year of the program, 74 percent of these children received scores that were average or above average. The Arkansas Hippy program has been so successful that it has been replicated throughout the state. Parents have become more involved in their children's school work and have been motivated to further their own education.

Reference

The Barbara Bush Foundation for Family Literacy. (1989). Arkansas Home Instruction Program for Preschool Youngsters (HIPPY). In *First Teachers* (pp. 32–34). Washington, DC: Author.

Bilingual Family Libraries
Chicago, Illinois

Program Description ❖ In a partnership with Reading Is Fundamental (RIF), the Chicago Commons Association (CCA) piloted the Bilingual Family Libraries program at two community centers operated by CCA that serve low-income Hispanic families. CCA reaches these families through two settlement houses: Emerson House and Taylor House. A wide range of human services are offered, including a Head Start and emergency food and clothing. Bilingual Family Libraries is centered around the development of an informal lending library at each center, free book distributions, workshops, and special literacy events. An advisory committee composed of parents, CCA staff, and Vista/ACTION volunteers designs and operates this program.

The committee initially stocked shelves with some 700 books in Spanish and English ranging from preschool to adult reading levels. Several hundred more volumes were purchased the next year. A kick-off event was held at Taylor House in 1988 that featured a professional storyteller and two plays. Children were invited to choose and keep free books. Students from the local Erikson Institute worked with the advisory committee to design a series of four workshops entitled "Children and Parents Reading Together." These workshops covered such topics as precursors to reading, how children learn to read, selecting good books, and the importance of reading to children. Average attendance for each session was eight. Each participant received pamphlets, a certificate of participation, an application for a public library card, and an orientation to the center's own home lending library.

After resolving some problems with lending procedures, the Taylor House Library reopened in May 1989, as did the Emerson House Library later in the month. With each reopening, the advisory committee launched a reading incentive that has proved very popular. For each book they read children are awarded stickers, which are collected on sticker cards. A stuffed toy may be selected upon filling up a card. Parents receive monthly hand-outs about reading, and a family reading club is being planned.

Program Success ❖ The pilot's success is evident in the improved attitudes toward reading observed at the two libraries, increased offerings, and future activities planned by the committee.

Reference
Reading Is Fundamental (1991). Bilingual Family Libraries. In *A guide to RIF's family literacy programs* (pp. 60–63). Washington, DC: Author.

Bilingual Programme
Pajaro Valley School District
California

Program Description ❖ The Bilingual Programme of the Pajaro Valley School District serves a rural population of about 15,000 students, 54 percent of whom are Hispanic, mostly Mexican. Twenty-nine percent are migrants, and 34.5 percent do not yet speak English. Since 1986, participant children's parents, most of whom have had very limited formal education, meet once a month with teachers to discuss children's literature and stories they and their children have written. Readings are followed by a question and answer period plus a dialogue that consists of four phases: (1) descriptive—in which information is set forth, (2) personal-interpretive—in which reactions and feelings about the reading are discussed, (3) critical—in which critical analysis of events and ideas present within the story takes place, and (4) creative—in which the reading is discussed in terms of discovering a real-life application. All activities are conducted in Spanish due to the underlying beliefs that language skills are best learned in one's native language, that a well-developed home language is the best basis for the acquisition of a second language, and that literacy is not defined by knowledge of English.

Program Success ❖ Participant parents have taken up reading to their children at home and discussing books. Personal growth occurred in both parents and children; relationships improved; and parents have more courage and self-esteem, which motivate them to become more involved in school activities.

Reference
Ada, A.F. (1988). The Pajaro Valley experience: Working with Spanish-speaking parents to develop children's reading and writing skills in the home through the use of children's literature. In T. Moreover-Kangas & J. Cummins (Eds.), *Minority education: From shame to struggle*. Philadelphia, PA: Multilingual Matters.

Center for Family Life
Brooklyn, New York

Program Description ❖ In 1989, Reading Is Fundamental (RIF) launched a family literacy program at the Center for Family Life in Brooklyn, New York. The center provides family-centered activities and counseling for low-income residents of the Sunset Park area. The children served attend the public schools with the lowest reading and math scores in the district. This RIF program takes place after school twice a week, from 3:00 to 4:30 p.m. Children aged 5 to 16 bring their families to the center. The children are read aloud to by specialists while their mothers, fathers, grandparents, older siblings, or other relatives are taught how to help their younger family members acquire the skills they need to succeed in school and how to share literacy skills. Child care for very young children is provided so that mothers are free to participate. Parents are very involved in the management of the program, helping with book selections, distributions, and fundraising. The center also instituted a system of pairing younger and older children for various cross-age reading activities when RIF books are distributed. Children in fifth and sixth grade read new books to younger children for 45 minutes. Then the younger children get to take home their new books. The center also offers a newsletter that features children's reviews of RIF books, poems, articles, and artwork.

Program Success ❖ Reading in the home as well as parent and family involvement in children's education has improved the lives of participants.

Reference

Reading Is Fundamental. (1991). Center for Family Life. In *A guide to RIF's family literacy programs* (pp. 35–36). Washington, DC: Author.

Central Vermont Community Action Council
Barre, Vermont

Program Description ❖ This program is run through Reading Is Fundamental (RIF) and is a home-based Head Start program. Home visitors make weekly visits to the homes of some 200 low-income families in three rural communities of Vermont. The children receive RIF books, which are frequently integrated with prescribed Head Start activities. The home visitors show parents how ordinary home activities and objects can be used to develop children's language as well as social and cognitive skills. For example, the home visitor may demonstrate how sorting socks teaches children how to classify and how setting a table illustrates words that indicate spatial relationships. The home visitors are trained to be alert to ways in which RIF books can be linked to developmental activities. They are also required to demonstrate nutrition activities and to take the opportunity to introduce relevant children's books to the families. Parents are required to serve on the Head Start Council, thereby offering them the opportunity for active involvement.

Program Success ❖ Parents and children alike have been delighted by the RIF books and related activities.

Reference

Reading Is Fundamental. (1991). Central Vermont Community Action Council. In *A guide to RIF's family literacy programs* (pp. 27–28). Washington, DC: Author.

Children and Books
Okemos, Michigan

Program Description ❖ Children and Books was an 18-week class (2 1/2 hours a week) taught by a program supervisor at the Haslett Family Learning Center in Okemos, Michigan. The objectives were threefold: (1) to entice pregnant and parenting teenagers into reading by presenting information of interest on the subject of raising children, (2) to familiarize the students with the wide array of books and magazines available as resource guides, and (3) to introduce children's books that are appropriate to various developmental stages.

The instructor compiled used paperbacks and magazines to create a "bookstore" where students could purchase reading materials at a nominal price. At the beginning of the program, students were invited to participate in a discussion about their memories of favorite childhood books. However, it turned out that most of the participants had never been read to as children. Then wordless picture books for the very young were introduced, and the mothers gave interpretations of the scenes. Here the class took an unexpected turn. Many told tales of domestic violence and assault. As storytellers they revealed events that some had never before discussed. This led to supportive bonding among class members and to referrals to outside sources of counseling. Students' children participated with their mothers for part of class time.

Program Success ❖ Mothers became avid users of the bookstore and made reading materials about parenting part of their everyday lives. By the end of the term, most of the mothers were comfortable reading to their children and had become familiar with a wide variety of books and resource materials. The instructor also reported that the students had come to believe in the intrinsic value of reading and in themselves as competent parents.

Reference

Doneson, S.G. (1991). Reading as a second chance: Teen mothers and children's books. *Journal of Reading, 35* (3), 220–222.

Club Familiar de Narracion de Cuentos
(Family Storytelling Club)
Washington, DC

Program Description ❖ Reading Is Fundamental (RIF) and the Spanish Education Development (SED) Center have sponsored this program. SED is a nonprofit, community-based organization that was founded in 1971 to assist Spanish-speaking immigrants, The Center is located in Adams Morgan, a low-income neighborhood that houses the majority of Washington D.C.'s 100,000 Hispanics. The Center also offers a preschool and classes in English as a second language. The goal of Club Familiar was to encourage low-literacy Hispanic families to read for pleasure, thereby increasing both their life skills and self-esteem. The program targeted families whose children attended the SED Center preschool.

Storytelling—a cultural, educational, and familiar activity—was chosen as the vehicle for reaching these families. The program's activities aimed to encourage parents to share their Latin-American traditions with their children. Props such as puppets and flannel boards were used to make the stories come to life. The program presented 14 sessions at the SED Center during the 15 months of the pilot program. Sessions included both storytelling and reading. The average attendance for each session was 34 children and 29 adults, with a total audience of 532 children and 387 adults. Additionally, six home sessions were hosted by parents. At first, parents were shy about actively participating in the program. By the end of the pilot, 18 parents had participated and more were lined up for future storytelling sessions. The coordinators of the program also offered three parent workshops on the importance of reading aloud to children and on how to use the 700-volume bilingual library that was created to provide stories for this program.

Program Success ❖ The program coordinators have described Club Familiar as an "unqualified success." Parents have become accustomed to the library, and its usage continues to increase. A survey of the participants at the end of the pilot showed that 47 percent of the parents would participate as storytellers in future programs—an increase of 25 percent from earlier responses. Eighty percent of the parents said that they would continue to attend, and 90 percent stated that it was very important for a parent to been seen as a storyteller by his or her child. The program received a State Award in the Family Circle/CPDA Leaders of Readers program. Interest in Club Familiar has extended nationally.

Reference

Reading Is Fundamental. (1991). Club Familiar de Narracion (Family Storytelling Club). In *A guide to RIF's family literacy programs* (pp. 48–50). Washington, DC: Author.

Dog Gone Good Reading Project
Virginia

Program Description ❖ This shared reading program for school and home was developed to assist teachers as they face the challenge of teaching growing numbers of culturally and linguistically diverse beginning readers. The program is currently being used in five Chapter 1 schools in a large suburban school district in the Washington, D.C., metropolitan area. Teachers in participating classrooms send books and audiotapes home on a daily basis to supplement the classroom reading instructional program. This provides an opportunity for students to hear English storybooks in their home environment using familiar literacy instructional materials from school.

To accommodate a range of interests and reading difficulty levels, over 150 natural language patterned books that have been used successfully in first-grade classrooms were selected for use. These books range in length from 14 words to complex narrative stories. To provide models of fluent reading in English, the program includes teachers' shared reading of the project books in the classroom and audiotapes of the stories for use in students' homes. In order to develop daily home reading routines, the project provides access to literacy materials (such as books, audiotapes, and tape recorders), training in procedures for their use, and regular communication with parents about the rereading activity.

Program Success ❖ Along with increased student interest in books, both teachers and parents observed a definite increase in children's fluency and reading independence. Furthermore, they noticed children beginning to monitor their reading.

References

Blum, I.H., Koskinen, P.S., Tennant, N., Parker, E.M., Straub, M., & Curry, C. (1994). *Developing Children's Fluency Through Shared Reading.* (Tech Rep.) College Park, MD: University of Maryland, National Reading Research Center.

Koskinen, P.S., Blum, I.H., Tennant, N., Parker, E.M., Straub, M., & Curry, C. (1995). Have you heard any good books lately? Using books and audiotapes to encourage shared reading at home. In L. Morrow (Ed.), *Family literacy connections in schools and communities.* Newark, DE: International Reading Association.

Family Reading Initiative
Chicago, Illinois

Program Description ❖ The Family Reading Initiative was a 15-month pilot program conducted by Reading Is Fundamental (RIF) in partnership with the Chicago Commons Association, a large social service agency serving five of Chicago's neediest West Side neighborhoods. This program was developed by Mile Square Community Center at the Henry Horner Homes public housing project to complement the center's Parent and Teen Support Services. These services include a Head Start program and a preschool. The Family Reading Initiative added a program of activities to promote reading motivation, which included home visitations, the installation of reading centers in participant families' homes, and workshops.

During regularly scheduled visits, a social worker and staff home visitor made house calls to participant families. They discussed the importance of reading and modeled reading activities. They also provided information on child care and homemaking skills. Home visitors introduced family members to early childhood development concepts and skills that lead to reading and language development using a new book that was especially selected for each family. Length of home visits ranged from 25 to 60 minutes. The number of visits varied, depending on each family's individual needs. In the 15-month period, 155 visits were conducted.

The program provided home reading centers for 23 families. The centers consisted of reading materials, a bookcase, and an area rug. The 23 recipient mothers ranged in age from 14 to 23 and were the parents of 40 children, 25 of whom were under the age of 3. These mothers had been invited to participate in the program based on their involvement and commitment to previous activities at the Center. When other parents heard about the reading centers, the number of requests began to far exceed what could be provided by program funds.

Program Success ❖ Anecdotal records show that reading has become an important part of the lives of the young parents who participated in the program. Children responded to the home visits with a sense of interest and excitement. The parents have demonstrated an improved ability to communicate their needs. The Family Reading Initiative was a Grand Prize winner in the 1989 Family Circle/CPDA Leaders of Readers Program.

Reference

Reading Is Fundamental. (1991). Family Reading Initiative. In *A guide to RIF's family literacy programs* (pp. 45–47). Washington, DC: Author.

From Day One
Albuquerque, New Mexico

Program Description ❖ From Day One takes place at New Futures School, an alternative public high school for teenage parents and pregnant teenagers. Over the last three terms, 150 students elected to take a children's literature course, and 10 became the torchbearers of From Day One, a peer outreach program designed to encourage parent involvement in literacy that was developed with a grant from Reading Is Fundamental (RIF). The children's literature course involves students in reading, reviewing, and making children's books. A special literacy event is sponsored for each term. These have included visits from a writer and an illustrator. The students in this class also design special reading packets that teach teen mothers how to stimulate their children's interest in reading. These packets come in a series for parents of newborns and for children's first and second birthdays. The newborn packets are distributed by visiting nurses on their first home visits following the birth of a child. A developmental aid in the school's nursery distributes the first-and second-year packets.

Program Success ❖ The participants leave with a great zeal for nurturing a love of books and reading in their children. They have developed positive feelings toward reading, in spite of their own past difficulties. This positive attitude forges a strong link in the chain of literacy.

Reference
Reading Is Fundamental. (1991). From Day One. In *A guide to RIF's family literacy programs* (pp. 55–57). Washington, DC: Author.

Gift Book Program
Pittsburgh, Pennsylvania

Program Description ❖ The Gift Book Program is offered through Beginning with Books, a nonprofit, early intervention literacy organization affiliated with the Carnegie Library of Pittsburgh. Low-income parents receive gift book packets through this program at homeless shelters, food banks, and well-baby clinics. The packets contain three high-quality children's books, suggestions on reading to children, and a coupon for another free book, to be redeemed at the local library. Participant parents are counseled on the importance of reading aloud regularly to their children in the early years. The target population consists of families with children between the ages of one and three.

Program Success ❖ Data suggest that parents who received the book packets read to their children and visited the library more frequently than they had before. Children in the study participated in listening to stories and showed an interest in reading in school. A greater percentage of children who received the gift book packets were rated in the top third of their class in reading and language ability at the kindergarten level than those who had not.

Reference

Bean, R.M., et al. (1990). *The Beginning with Books Gift Book Program: Effects on family and child literacy.* Paper presented at the Annual Meeting of the National Reading Conference (40th, Miami, FL). (ERIC Document Reproduction Service No. ED 329 926)

Knox County Head Start
Mount Vernon, Ohio

Program Description ❖ This Reading Is Fundamental program was founded in 1986 and operates at three sites: one in Danville, Ohio, and two in Mount Vernon, a rural farming area in Ohio. This program is offered to 100 low-income families of 140 Head Start participants, two-thirds of whom live with a single parent. The Knox County Head Start program sends trained parent educators into the homes of these families. The parent educator models by reading out loud and asking open-ended questions as the mother watches carefully. After the mother has observed these procedures several times, she is encouraged to try them herself. Books are left in the home every week for parents and children to read together. Parents are encouraged to allow the child to look through the book and talk about the story. The parents use an activity chart for bedtime stories. Every time a story is read, a happy face is recorded on the chart, which also contains suggestions for helping children develop a love of reading.

On a subsequent visit, the parent educator brings a flannel board, blunt scissors, construction paper, puppet patterns, and a felt-tip pen. The child cuts out and creates a paper figure and retells a now-familiar story in his or her own words. The parent educators give parents guidance on the appropriate way to respond to and provide praise for the child's efforts. Throughout the week the parent helps the child retell stories using the flannel board. To prepare for the next visit, the parent educator asks the child to make up a story that will be shared.

Program Success ❖ This program succeeds in helping children understand that symbols can communicate thoughts and feelings. It opens the door to the magical world of books while training parents how to be actively involved in literacy activities.

Reference

Reading Is Fundamental. (1991). Knox County Head Start. In *A guide to RIF's family literacy programs* (pp. 23–24). Washington, DC: Author.

Marquette University Family Literacy Project
Wisconsin

Program Description ❖ This project is a partnership between Marquette University and two elementary schools. The overall goals are to improve the quality of education available to children and families in the neighborhoods near the campus and to provide training and experience for preservice and inservice teachers. The partnership schools are both private, parent-operated schools. The majority of children qualify for free or reduced lunch programs. The Family Literacy Project's first year of operation was the 1993–1994 school year. The project offers tutoring in reading and writing for children, information and experiences designed to help parents support their children's literacy development, supervised training for undergraduate and graduate education students, as well as a continuing education program in literacy education for teachers in the partnership schools.

Program Success ❖ Children participating in the twice per week tutoring program made significant gains in reading: ninety-eight percent improved at least one instructional reading level as measured by informal reading assessment techniques. Sixty-one percent made gains of two to four reading levels. Growth in reading was positively correlated with the amount of independent reading the children did at home in project-provided materials. Parent participation varied from none to full. Sixty-four percent of families participated in at least one event. One hundred percent of parents who filled out end of year questionnaires reported that they would recommend the project to other families.

Reference

Allen, L., & Leslie, L. (1994). The Marquette Family Literacy Project: An Integrated Model. *Wisconsin State Reading Association Journal, 38* (2), 15–20.

Missouri Parents as Teachers (PAT)
St. Louis, Missouri

Program Description ❖ The Missouri Parents as Teachers (PAT) was founded by the State of Missouri in 1981 to give extra help to low-income families with preschool children. This program sends parent educators trained at the University of Missouri to the homes of at-risk families to help ensure that more children enter kindergarten prepared to learn. PAT centers are housed in elementary and secondary schools and employ a full- or part-time coordinator as well as full- or part-time parent educators. Approximately 9 to 13 parent educators, each responsible for some 60 families, work out of each center. Visits are scheduled at intervals of four to six weeks, and group meetings are held monthly. Licensed teachers are recruited by local school districts to work as parent educators. They are trained to help parents stimulate their children's physical, social, and cognitive development. Their credentials must be renewed each year for five years, after which time they receive "tenure."

In 1990, Reading Is Fundamental (RIF) piloted RIF programs at four PAT Early Infant Centers in the city of St. Louis. Each of the four centers supports 600 families. RIF's efforts to distribute books to children at an early age works well with PAT's emphasis on language development and reading aloud to children. RIF books are delivered to participant families at the PAT centers and during home visits. Three distributions per year are provided and include nursery rhyme and poetry books, brightly colored alphabet books, and counting books. During home visits, parents are taught the importance of reading out loud and reinforcing their child's development through games and play that are developmentally appropriate. Parent educators also teach parents how to make books and toys.

Program Success ❖ Parent educators have reported that because of the easy availability of RIF books, parents are reading more to their children. The program is also motivating parents to continue their own education.

Reference

Reading Is Fundamental. (1991). Missouri Parents as Teachers. In *A guide to RIF's family literacy programs* (pp. 25–26). Washington, DC: Author.

Navajo Parent Child Reading Program
Arizona

Program Description ❖ The Navajo Parent Child Reading Program was initiated in 1985 at the Chinle Primary School on the Navajo Reservation in Arizona. Children's literature is used to bridge the gap between school and home cultures. Stories are read to preschoolers at the school in both Navajo and English. The children are then encouraged to take the books home and share the stories, via retellings, with their parents, many of whom do not read well in either Navajo or English. Parents are encouraged to tell stories using oral tradition and customs. Although this program does not emphasize reading of the actual text, literacy behavior and enjoyment of books are fostered. Videos that demonstrate enjoyment of books in both Navajo and English are made available to parents.

Program Success ❖ Children have demonstrated enjoyment of the readings that take place every day, as well as excitement in sharing the books with their families. Parents have come to know that written stories are akin to Navajo oral tales and have become more active in school affairs.

Reference
Viola, M., et al. Report on the Navajo Parent Child Reading Program at the Chinle Primary School. Chinle School District, Chinle, Arizona.

Parent Leadership Training Project
Washington State

Program Description ❖ The Parent Leadership Training Project, a pilot program that began in 1986, was conducted by the Citizens' Education Center Northwest in cooperation with the Washington State Migrant Council in the Yakima Valley area of Washington State. The program was designed to meet the needs of area Chicano/Latino parents, whose children have a high school dropout rate of 86 percent. The goal is to help parents and children make a successful transition from preschool to public school kindergarten by encouraging parents to have early involvement in their children's education. The goal is also to help lower the school dropout rate in the long run. The program has been successfully replicated with parents of children in grades K–5. Project sites are located at Washington State Migrant Council Preschool Centers in Sunnyside and Mabton, Washington, and in the Wapato and Toppenish school districts and at an elementary school in Seattle.

This program provides a series of 14 parent training sessions, to which principals, teachers, and other administrators are invited. Child care is provided. Topics covered include information on what children learn in preschool, how to reinforce children's school skills during the summer, parent-teacher relations, student testing, how to read a report card and how to help children read even if the parent cannot read (for example, using wordless books). As an additional component, English as a second language (ESL) classes are provided by other community agencies.

Program Success ❖ Participant parents have become more involved in their children's school work and either read or have someone read to their children in the home on a regular basis. Parents also visit libraries.

Reference

The Barbara Bush Foundation for Family Literacy. Parent Leadership Training Project. In *First teachers* (pp. 46–48). Washington, DC: Author.

The Parent Resource Center
Graterford Prison
Graterford, Pennsylvania

Program Description ❖ In 1987 a prisoner at Graterford Prison (for men) in Pennsylvania wrote to Reading Is Fundamental (RIF) about starting a family literacy program in the prison. Later that year, RIF launched a program at Graterford in tandem with the prison's Parent Resource Center (PRC), which had already been in operation for two years. This program offers prison fathers a chance to give books to their children and nurture their reading skills. The PRC is dedicated to supporting the father-child relationship and, as part of the RIF program, offers workshops to teach fathers how to read out loud to their children. These workshops also demonstrate how to design activities that will attract children to books, such as flannel board stories and puppet shows. Initial purchasing funds came from the fathers' prison wages.

On a RIF visiting day, children line up at the PRC to select a book to be read with their families. Volunteer inmates help with book distribution. Other inmates present puppet shows or flannel board stories based on children's classics. Visiting time, which had previously been a typically stressful occasion, has been transformed into a literacy-centered, enjoyable experience.

Program Success ❖ RIF reports that "judging by its ability to galvanize interest in children's reading and bring prisoners and their families together to improve their children's literacy skills, the Graterford RIF project is an unqualified success."

Reference

Reading Is Fundamental. (1991). The Parent Resource Center, Graterford Prison. In *A guide to RIF's family literacy programs* (pp. 17–20). Washington, DC: Author.

Parents as Partners in Reading
Donaldsonville, Kentucky

Program Description ❖ The Parents as Partners in Reading program seeks to improve the literacy rate among socioeconomically deprived families by teaching parents how to read to their children. The program is set in the elementary school library in Donaldsonville, Louisiana, and has been replicated at Withrow School in Springfield, Illinois. The program takes place for two hours a week throughout the school year, beginning in August and ending in May.

Participants view videotapes of outstanding teachers and staff modeling good reading behavior. Ongoing tapes are created, showing program parents reading to their children. Parents are taught successful story comprehension strategies such as connecting a book with previous knowledge that children may have, asking questions, making comparisons, and developing other thinking skills. Participants are also lent books from the school library to practice reading at home with their children.

Program Success ❖ Teachers of participant children have reported an improvement in student achievement in the elementary school, and teacher morale has improved because of better communication with parents. Parents have reported that book reading has become an important part of their daily lives.

Reference

The Barbara Bush Foundation for Family Literacy. (1989). Parents as Partners in Reading. In *First teachers* (pp. 40–42). Washington, DC: Author.

Parents as Tutors (PAT)
Brownsville, Texas

Program Description ❖ This program began in 1984 and is funded by Title VII. It serves the families of limited-English-proficiency (LEP) students in kindergarten through second grade in Brownsville, Texas. Eighty percent of the parents are predominantly or entirely Spanish speaking and come from Mexico. The program has three goals: to increase parent involvement, to improve self-concept, and to increase children's academic achievement. In the first year, tutoring focuses on generic activities for all parents to conduct at home. These activities focus on language arts and mathematics. During the second year, when the children are in the first grade, the parents (who are provided with child care and transportation) meet bi-weekly. They participate in discussion sessions that alternate between informational topics and the development of activities for home tutoring. During the third year, continued parent training takes place and a training manual is developed.

Program Success ❖ The effectiveness of this program was monitored through questionnaires completed by the parents. Many of the parents who participate in PAT go on to study English as a second language, and some have received their GEDs.

Reference

Sandoval, M. (1986). Issues of parent involvement and literacy. Proceedings of a symposium (pp. 89–90). Washington, DC: Trinity College.

Parents Sharing Books
Bloomington, Indiana

Program Description ❖ Parents Sharing Books was developed by the Family Literacy Center at Indiana University in Bloomington as a way to help parents become involved in reading with their middle-school children. Research indicates that students lose interest in books during their pre-teen years and that parents are still powerful role models at this stage. This program is designed as an intervention to keep preteens interested in reading and to increase interaction between these youngsters and their parents. A secondary goal is to ease the parent-child relationship, which can often be strained at this stage, by reading young adult books that address issues that are often of concern to preteens.

In the fall of 1990, Lily Endowment, Inc., targeted specific schools in Indiana where the socioeconomic status of the residents was low and the population was dense. Twenty-three schools applied to participate in the program. Leader teams, each consisting of one parent and one teacher, attended two days' training at Indiana University on a scholarship. A training package was developed for the leader teams to use in training other parents. The package included information on early adolescence and books, motivation, books appropriate for this age group, and how to help leader teams start programs at the local level.

Program Success ❖ Evaluation data collected in the first year focused on the training. Forty-nine percent of the leader teams rated the training seminars as excellent, 42 percent as very good, and 9 percent as good. Second-year data will focus on the changes that have taken place between parents participating in the program and their children.

Reference

Smith, C.B. (1991). *Parents Sharing Books. Annual report, 1990–1991.* Bloomington Indiana University, Family Literacy Center. (ERIC Document Reproduction Service No. ED 335 645)

Preparing Refugees for Elementary Programs (PREP)
Washington, DC

Program Description ❖ This program involves elementary school children and their parents and is run by the Philippines Refugee Processing Center. Many of the participants are from Indochina. PREP functions on a 20-week cycle. Each cycle begins with an "open house," an informal get-together for parents, teachers, and children. Orientation to PREP and to the elementary school system is provided. During the third week, a PTA is formed, followed by a parent-teacher conference. Each cycle also includes an evening parent-teacher social hour and two or three home visits by the teacher. Throughout each cycle, teachers encourage the parents to participate in the classrooms. Parents tutor, teach native songs, cook native food, and decorate the classroom. They are allowed to use their own ideas about how they would like to participate. PREP also encourages parent participation in homework assignments designed to involve family members. Each cycle ends with a graduation that everyone involved is encouraged to attend.

Program Success ❖ PREP succeeds in helping to demystify a new educational system that can be intimidating to immigrant parents. The program's use of native languages and cultures in the classroom has proven to be an effective way to bring about involvement of parents who would otherwise lack the confidence to participate in school-related activities.

Reference

Ranard, D.A. (1989). *Family literacy: Trends and practices.* Center for Applied Linguistics, Washington, DC. Bureau of Refugee Programs. (ERIC Document Reproduction Service No. ED 323 754)

Project Home Base
Yakima, Washington

Program Description ❖ Project Home Base, located in Yakima, Washington, the "fruit capital of the world," serves many migrant families. The program sends parent educators weekly into the homes of 180 low-income families in the local school district. They teach parents about early childhood development and health care, while helping youngsters to develop the skills and confidence needed to enter school prepared to learn. Families are frequently referred by the Department of Health and Social Services. To qualify for participation, the family must reside in a Yakima Chapter 1 school neighborhood and have a child from one to five years old who is at risk for developmental delays. Parents and children are screened in their homes to determine the child's developmental level, home environment, and parents' skill level. Reading Is Fundamental provides books three times a year to participant families to complement Project Home Base's goal of introducing books to children during their formative years and teaching parents how to conduct reading readiness events at home. The parent educators, who are familiar with individual children's tastes and reading levels, select the appropriate books.

Program Success ❖ Project Home Base is an inexpensive and successful approach to helping children prepare for success in school. Participant parents are active later on in their children's school activities, PTAs, and as volunteers in school. This, in turn, supports children's academic success.

Reference
Reading Is Fundamental. (1991). Project Home Base. In *A guide to RIF's family literacy programs* (pp. 29–30). Washington, DC: Author.

Project ROAR (Reach Out and Read)
Boston, Massachusetts

Program Description ❖ Project ROAR (Reach Out and Read) was started by three pediatricians on the Boston City Hospital staff. This program serves clients out of the hospital's primary care clinics. In conjunction with Reading Is Fundamental (RIF), ROAR serves 2,500 children aged 3 to 5 and their families all year around; 95 percent of these families are from low-income and minority groups.

When families come to the clinics, they are greeted by a volunteer foster grandparent who asks "who wants to hear a story?" The volunteer models reading-aloud behavior for the parents and asks the children questions to stimulate their interest. After the child's medical visit, the pediatrician explains to the parents how important it is to read to their children daily. Before the family departs, the doctor offers their choice of a children's book. RIF helps to provide these books, which make their way into the homes of some of the poorest families in Boston. Parents also receive colorful bookmarks, tips on how to read to children, and charts showing appropriate activities for various ages. Volunteers show the parents that they need not be skilled readers themselves to share books with their children. They are told about the importance of talking and are shown how to make up stories and ask questions to involve children in the reading and storytelling process.

Program Success ❖ Many participant parents now read to their children when they are in the hospital. Parent workshops have also been started to encourage active participation in children's reading.

Reference

Reading Is Fundamental. (1991). Project ROAR. In *A guide to RIF's family literacy programs* (pp. 15–16). Washington, DC: Author.

Reading Together
Bryan, Texas

Program Description ❖ Reading Together began in 1988 as a community program that aims to encourage families to read with their children. Reading Is Fundamental (RIF) sponsored this pilot, working with various public agencies and community volunteers to design and conduct a 15-month multimedia campaign to target disadvantaged and minority families. Low-income, low-literacy minority families—an equal percentage of African Americans and Hispanics—make up 44 percent of Bryan, Texas' 52,000 residents. The Reading Together program hoped to raise parental awareness in Bryan of the importance of reading with children. In addition to seed money provided by RIF, community leaders helped significantly with donations of both money and services. Students from the nearby Texas A&M University offered volunteer services.

The program sponsored, as an initial effort, a billboard contest in which over 2,600 children (K–6th grades) participated. Two hundred children received prizes, and the three grand-prize winners had their artwork enlarged and displayed on billboards along heavily traveled street in the area for 30 months, promoting the family literacy message. Some of the contest entries were reproduced on postcards and T-shirts that were sold to raise additional program funds.

Additionally, book boxes were placed in many high traffic "sit and wait" spots such as laundromats, the Health Department, and the prenatal clinic. Parents and children were free to use the books and even borrow them. A "sports book rally" was sponsored by the local telephone company for 850 5th graders. This was actually a reading motivation rally that included a pep talk about reading, special cheerleading, a performance by the junior high school band, and free books and posters for everyone. Public service announcements promoting reading together were aired on the radio and television, and a seven-minute video offering tips on reading to children was made. The Reading Together program also provided children's books to adults enrolled in literacy classes and provided three children's books to each new mother at the local hospital.

Program Success ❖ Reading Together has been very successful in all respects. All the events in the program attracted overwhelming public attention and engendered both interest and support. The original grant was doubled due to cash contributions; a new pool of volunteers has been activated to continue with other family literacy activities in the community.

Reference
Reading Is Fundamental. (1991). Reading Together. In *A guide to RIF's family literacy programs* (pp. 69–71). Washington, DC: Author.

Ready for Reading
Southern Illinois

Program Description ❖ The Ready for Reading program is located in southern Illinois and uses the existing network of family service providers to recruit participants. This program provides parents with the skills and beginning materials needed to encourage reading with their young children. Three two-hour sessions are conducted with the parents at the child's school while the children are in Pre-K classes. Parents are made aware of the significance of stressing the importance of reading to their children. The program provides the parents with a packet of three children's books, a guide with easy-to-make home activities, pamphlets, a calendar, and a coupon for an additional book to be redeemed at their local library. The instructors teach strategies to use with children and discuss appropriate times for reading, how to read to children, and how to involve children in the story. Because many of the parents have low-level reading skills, alternative ways of sharing books are also presented.

Program Success ❖ The program showed more evidence of success where it was able to network with a Pre-K provider that was already established and accepted in the local community. Family literacy teachers operating in communities with newly established Pre-K programs have had a more difficult time recruiting participants for the program. The original curriculum was outlined to proceed first with publicity and recruitment followed by parent sessions, book distribution, home and library visits, and finally in-class follow-up sessions.

One location successfully began with the in-class sessions in order to recruit parents. Other teachers have rearranged their components successfully.

Reference

Bauernfeind, B. (1990). *Ready for reading: A community college approach to family literacy.* Paper presented at the annual meeting of the American Reading Forum (11th, Sarasota, FL). (ERIC Document Reproduction Service No. ED 329 916)

Running Start: A Reading Motivation Program for First Graders Nationwide

Program Description ❖ The Running Start (RS) program is a school-based project designed to get books into the hands of first grade children and to encourage and support family literacy. Running Start was created by Reading Is Fundamental (RIF) under a grant from the Chrysler Corporation Fund. The three primary goals of the RS program are (1) to increase first graders' motivation to read so they eagerly turn to books for both pleasure and information, (2) to involve parents in their children's literacy development, and (3) to support schools and teachers in their efforts to help children become successful readers. Participating classroom teachers are provided with funds to select and purchase high quality fiction and informational books for the classroom library. Children are challenged to read (or have someone read to them) 21 books during the 10-week program. A Reading Rally is held to involve the community in supporting literacy development, and parents are encouraged to support their child in meeting the 21-book challenge by sharing books and stories with their children in a variety of ways. When a child meets the 21-book goal, he or she gets to select a book for his or her own personal library.

Program Success ❖ More than 7,000 children, their parents, and their teachers participated in a national evaluation of the RS program. The comparison of pretest and posttest indicated that the RS program resulted in statistically significant increases in first grader's reading motivation and engagement in literacy tasks as well as parents' involvement in literacy activities in the home environment. A second study, using a quasi-experimental design, conducted with children and families from minority backgrounds also reveals statistically significant gains in first graders' motivation to read and in family literacy practices. A third study was conducted during second grade with the children involved in the quasi-experimental study, and it documented that the program supports and sustains literacy development beyond the 10-week duration of the actual program.

References

For more information see Gambrell, L.B., Almasi, J.F., Xie, Q., & Heland, W. (1995). Helping first graders get off to a Running Start in reading: A home-school-community program that enhances family literacy. In L. M. Morrow (Ed.) *Family literacy connections in schools and communities.* Newark, DE: International Reading Association. If you would like to be put on the mailing list for information about Running Start, send requests to Running Start Mailing List, Reading Is Fundamental, 600 Maryland Ave., S.W., Suite 600, Washington, DC 20024, or FAX: 202–287–3196.

Shared Beginnings
Nationwide

Program Description ❖ In 1990, Reading Is Fundamental (RIF) received a grant from the New York Life Foundation to expand its work with teen parents and their children. Shared Beginnings was developed and field tested at 11 sites across the United States, beginning in January 1991. Sites that already offered services that drew teen parents together were chosen. These included residential homes for abused teenagers and their children, community health centers and alternative and traditional high schools. Parents and their infants and toddlers took part in Shared Beginnings, a program that provides teen parents with hands-on activities to help them learn how to develop their children's emergent literacy skills and teaches them how to employ literacy as a vehicle through which strong parent-child bonds can be developed. The frequency and length of program sessions varied to meet the curriculum needs of each individual site. At all locations, parents had access to their children for group activities that specifically included them. At the beginning of the program, parents receive an Idea Book, which provides parenting tips and home-based activities to complement the program.

Shared Beginnings is built around group activities, including talking, singing, rhyming, rocking, drawing, book-making, toy-making, and storytelling. As in all RIF programs, the participants have an opportunity to select three books to keep.

Program Success ❖ The pilot coordinators have provided rich anecdotal evidence that Shared Beginnings has improved the quality of nurturing received by participant children. They have also noted that the parents became impressed with the importance of reading and developed fine book selection skills. They also began to read out loud to their children more frequently than they had prior to participation in Shared Beginnings.

Reference

Reading Is Fundamental. (1991). Shared Beginnings. In *A guide to RIF's family literacy programs* (pp. 77–80). Washington, DC: Author.

Sock City Readers Club
Mount Airy, North Carolina

Program Description ❖ Sock City Readers Club is a Reading Is Fundamental (RIF) parent involvement family literacy program that is run in conjunction with an intergenerational program. It is operated by four sock-making hosiery mills in a small industrial town called Mount Airy, North Carolina. The mills established a small lending library of children's books in each of their eight break rooms (totaling 2,000 volumes). The personnel managers of the mills supervise the libraries and also coordinate adult literacy programs for the workers. A volunteer program coordinator offers on-site coursework toward the GED. Jointly, the mills have also sponsored free book distributions for the employees and their families.

Because children are not allowed on factory grounds, special weekend reading events were held at the local public library for workers and their children and grandchildren. Events have included making puppets from socks donated by the mills and listening to a professional storyteller. At all such events, children were invited to choose and keep a paperback book. These weekend activities became so popular that they were given their own identity and became a RIF pilot, Sock City Readers Club, in June 1989. More than 200 children enrolled as members and received membership cards, club T-shirts, and a reading log that could be redeemed for prizes. The mill coordinators were so impressed with the goodwill and enthusiasm engendered by RIF's Sock City Readers that they convinced company management to contribute funds that would make the pilot an ongoing program.

Program Success ❖ There are many indications that this program has raised the consciousness of the community regarding the importance of literacy. The mills have pledged to support the project and the break room libraries indefinitely. Numerous local businesses have made donations to support Sock City Readers.

Reference

Reading Is Fundamental. (1991). Sock City Readers. In *A guide to RIF's family literacy programs* (pp. 51–54). Washington, DC: Author.

A Story To Go
Ohio

Program Description ❖ Designed by an Ohio Chapter 1 reading teacher, A Story To Go gets parents involved in their child's reading and ultimately enhances family literacy. Students select from a variety of books and complete accompanying activities after they read their book. Parents are encouraged to become involved by reading the book to or with the child, depending on the book's level of difficulty. In some cases the book may be read entirely by the child, involving the parent as the listener. Activities vary across the curriculum from writing about the story to drawing a picture, making a book, or creating an art project.

The program's goals include getting children excited about reading a variety of literature, getting parents involved in their child's reading, and enhancing family literacy. Both the reading of the story and the related activity are done at home and are then brought to school to be shared with the teacher and others in the class.

Program Success ❖ A Story To Go gives children support for and the ability to internalize experiences they may have already had, which increases comprehension skills, It also provides new experiences for the child to relate to and identify with. This program challenges children to become lifelong readers and, with parental support, provides an opportunity for parent and child to enjoy a reading and writing experience together.

Success is also evident in children's desire to share stories and in their improvement in reading ability across the curriculum. Also children's self-evaluation of their reading has yielded the sorts of good feelings that are important in enhancing family literacy.

Reference

Marilyn J. Vaughan, Chapter 1 Coordinator, Logan Elm Local Schools. PO Box 234, Kingston, Ohio 45644. For more information call 614–642–2819.

Intergenerational Programs

INTERGENERATIONAL FAMILY LITERACY INITIA-
TIVES ARE DESIGNED TO IMPROVE THE LITERACY DEVEL-
OPMENT OF BOTH CHILDREN AND THEIR PARENTS. PAR-
ENTS AND CHILDREN ARE VIEWED AS CO-LEARNERS, AND
INSTRUCTION CAN TAKE PLACE WHEN PARENTS AND CHIL-
DREN WORK IN EITHER COLLABORATIVE OR PARALLEL SET-
TINGS. ADULTS ARE TAUGHT TO IMPROVE THEIR LITERA-
CY SKILLS AS WELL AS HOW TO WORK WITH THEIR
CHILDREN TO FOSTER THEIR LITERACY.

Avance Family Support and Education Program
San Antonio, Texas

Program Description ❖ This program was established in 1973 by a teacher to help reduce the disproportionately high dropout rate among Mexican-American children on the west side of San Antonio, Texas. Avance, which means "advancement" in Spanish, was designed to help children succeed in school by teaching parents to teach their children and by meeting adults' basic literacy and parenting needs. Avance was modeled after the former Parent-Child Development Centers. The first Avance Center opened at the Mirasol Federal Housing Project in San Antonio. Several other programs have since been established in other housing projects, converted day-care centers, churches, and community centers. Funding has been provided by such sources as the city of San Antonio, United Way, and private contributions.

For parents, Avance offers community-based workshops to develop parenting skills and help build home-school relationships; a Fatherhood Project, which involves fathers in special family-strengthening activities; a homebound education program to help abusive parents; basic literacy instruction; and classes on how to teach children basic skills. In these classes, parents also learn how they can make their own books and toys at home and how to use the library. Instructors' home visits reinforce what is learned in class. Videotaping is used for self-evaluation, and community resource awareness activities are provided.

Program Success ❖ Upon completion of this program, there is an increase in enrollment in adult education classes. Parents express an increased interest and involvement in their children's education and school activities. They also make more use of community resources.

Reference

The Barbara Bush Foundation for Family Literacy. (1989). Avance Family Support and Education Program. In *First teachers* (pp. 49–52). Washington, DC: Author.

The Collaborations and Literacy Model
The Family Literacy Center, Boston University
Boston, Massachusetts

Program Description ❖ The program is held at the Family Literacy Center at Boston University and is supervised and staffed by graduate students and faculty of the School of Education. The participants are recruited in cooperation with the Boston Public Schools, and the focus is on parents of Chapter 1 children. One-on-one tutoring is provided. Most of the participants are Hispanic, African American, and Asian, and most are women. The program operates under a four-step model: (1) tutors design a lesson plan (demonstration, guided practice, independent practice, and evaluation) with a focus on decoding, vocabulary, and reading and listening comprehension; (2) tutors model learning activities for parents to practice at home; (3) literacy events ("socials" for parents and children concerning shared reading and home activities) are provided; (4) weekly in-service sessions for tutors (on such topics as teaching strategies) are provided.

Program Success ❖ Reading gains on vocabulary and comprehension skills have been found, in correspondence with the increasing number of hours of tutoring. The retention rate has been 73 percent.

Reference
Nickse, R.S., et al. (1988). An intergenerational adult literacy project: A family prevention model. *Journal of Reading*, 635–641.

The El Paso Family Literacy for Parents of Pre-Schoolers Project
El Paso, Texas

Program Description ❖ This program is clustered around four Family Literacy Centers that impact 7 of the 14 Head Start Centers in the El Paso County Head Start Program in Texas. The program is designed to establish centers that could address the needs of parents whose children are about to enter neighborhood schools. It involves

118 parents of Head Start children. The major focus of the program is to educate parents. They attend a two-and-a-half hour class each week on parenting skills and the English language. Additionally, they receive assignments to enable them to apply these skills in the home environment with their children. The program works to improve the English language and literacy skills of the parents. Both the ESL and parenting skills classes include family literacy activities. The classes, which are composed of 16 sessions, are scheduled in the mornings and afternoons to accommodate parents' schedules. The parents also attend field trips to the university, local hospitals, and local banks during the year.

Program Success ❖ Thirty-two percent of the parents surveyed at the beginning of the program reported that they read to their children every night or at least once a week. At the end of the 16 weeks, this figure rose to 93 percent.

Reference
Enriquez, B., et al. (1990). *Family literacy for parents of preschoolers: A Title VII first-year evaluation report.* (ERIC Document Reproduction Service No. ED 337 056)

Families for Literacy, Project Read
Redwood City, California

Program Description ❖ Families for Literacy is a library sponsored, home-based literacy program for parents who want to read to their young children. Families can join if at least one parent is reading at or below the seventh grade level and the family has at least one kindergarten or preschool-aged child. The design is based on the observations that low-literate families do not frequently visit libraries, can feel uncomfortable when brought to one, and often find attending evening or weekend literacy activities inconvenient. Consequently, in this program the family and the tutor meet at the family's home.

The program is divided into three phases in which the family is gradually introduced to the library and encouraged to attend regularly scheduled story hours at the library with their tutor. Throughout the program, tutoring continues at the family's home.

Program Success ❖ This program has an 85% retention rate. Parents are tested every 6 months to determine their reading improvement. A research study that measured the progress of seven families showed increased test scores for both parent and child as well as improved attitudes and behaviors toward reading and reading to children. Families visited the library more frequently and attended more library sponsored story hours. The parents reported reading more often to their children and scheduling a regular story time.

Reference
Hansen, M.D. *Evaluation of an intergenerational model to improve family literacy.* California State University, Hayward.

For information contact David Miller, Director
Project Read
1044 Middlefield Road
Redwood City, CA 94063.

Families Reading Together: A Community–Supported Parent Tutoring Program
Philadelphia, Pennsylvania

Program Description ❖ Families Reading Together is designed on the principle of "investing in two generations at a time." Community leaders, supported by Americorp (formerly Vista Volunteers of America) recruit parents to participate in an early reading intervention for preschool, kindergarten, and pre-first grade children. The program is operated by Temple University in five North Philadelphia schools that serve primarily Latino and African-American families. Parents attend workshops to work on their own language and literacy development. They then provide tutoring to one or two children at a time in the school for 30–45 minutes twice a week. They use literacy prop boxes as intervention activities. Prop box materials are thematic-based activities that include: a chant, jingle or finger-play, a story-book, play objects based on the theme, and blank writing books.

The purpose of the program is not to supplant classroom instruction, but to provide additional opportunities for children to try out and practice reading and writing in a playful context. Unlike many other school interventions, however, the program is designed to encourage the community to help one another, empowering both parents and children to experience the confidence, joys, and power associated with literacy learning.

Program Success ❖ Now in its third year, Families Reading Together has significantly bolstered parent involvement in the schools. Over the past two years, 180 parents have regularly volunteered at least 2 hours a week to tutor young children most in need of additional intervention. Americorp leaders have collectively logged over 4,000 hours of reading to children as a result of parent efforts. In the course of these activities, both parents' and children's confidence in reading has continued to grow.

Community leaders have made over 88 literacy prop boxes for use in the schools. Due to their popularity, parents have created 198 boxes as take-home summer reading programs for children.

References

For more information contact Susan B. Neuman, Temple University, 437 Ritter Hall, Philadelphia, PA 19112.

The Family Initiative for English Literacy (FIEL)
El Paso, Texas

Program Description ❖ This three-year, school-based program helps limited English proficiency parents facilitate their own and their children's acquisition of English literacy skills. Classes are held in the child's classroom after dismissal from regular classes. FIEL is a five-step model for family literacy development run by the El Paso Community College Literacy Center. The philosophy that guides FIEL is that the command of reading and writing should be achieved through the use of themes that have meaning to those who are becoming educated, not just to the educators.

The goals of this program are (1) to enhance the literacy and biliteracy skills of both parents and children by providing models for literacy behavior through a series of participatory intergenerational activities; (2) to provide parents with information about children's literacy development; and (3) to empower parents to connect the literacy activities to their own lives and personal growth. Parents attend classes with their children for an hour once a week over twelve successive weeks in the fall and spring. The classes are facilitated by a teacher and assistant and are limited to a maximum of seven individuals per class.

FIEL was designed with the underlying premises that parent involvement has a positive effect on a child's life and that a holistic approach is more effective than a fragmented one. The "five-step model" refers to the five components of each lesson: initial inquiry, learning activity, language experience, storybook demonstration, and home assignment. The program curriculum consists of a series of lessons based on themes that have personal meaning to the participants. These include: puppets (a popular art form in Mexico), the extended family, recipes, holidays, cotton (cotton fields surround two of the schools), and the first Thanksgiving (as celebrated by the Spaniards in 1598).

Program Success ❖ Ethnographic studies conducted during the program's first year have offered evidence that FIEL has contributed significantly to the whole-life literacy behaviors of participant families.

Reference

Quintero, E., & Huerta-Macias, A. All in the family: Bilingualism and biliteracy. *The Reading Teacher, 44* (4), 306–312.

The Family Literacy Project: Focus on Teenage Parents
New York City

Program Description ❖ This project was developed by faculty in collaboration with the Board of Education's Living for Young Families through Education (LYFE). It is administered through Queens College and had been implemented at eight public high schools and one residential center. At each site the project is conducted by a faculty team comprising one classroom teacher and one member of the school's LYFE staff.

The project team works with teenage parents to engage them in activities that strengthen both their own literacy skills and their understanding of child development and parenting issues. The Project establishes a children's literature collection at each site that includes classics, Newbery and Caldecott selections, and multicultural titles. The Project sponsors a credit-bearing course, "Children's Literature," that requires students to read regularly to a young child, to keep a journal about these reading experiences, and to produce an original children's book. Class readings and discussions are organized around themes (for example, family, fairy tales, and folk tales).

Program Success ❖ The Project was selected by the American Association of Colleges for Teacher Education as an exemplar program for meeting the National Education Goals for the Year 2000. Participants showed improved reading comprehension on a cloze test and enriched understanding of parenting issues on the Parent Child Inventory. Teachers reported enhancement of students' positive attitudes toward reading and sense of self-efficacy.

Reference

American Association of Colleges for Teacher Education. (1992). Faculty and students provide services to elementary and secondary students. In *The National Education Goals: The AACTE Member Response* (p. 5). Washington, DC: American Association of Colleges for Teacher Education.

The Family WRAP Program: Writing and Reading Appreciation for Parents and Pupils
New Jersey

Program Description ❖ This is designed to bridge home and school literacy by engaging parents in developmentally appropriate and culturally sensitive literacy activities with their children. The purpose is to enhance both parent and child's achievement and attitudes toward reading and writing. The Family WRAP Program is a mirror image of the school WRAP Program, which is literature-based and includes literacy centers in classrooms containing books, writing materials, and literature manipulatives; teacher modeled literature activities; and periods of WRAP Time when children choose another student to work with on literacy activities. The home program has similar features to the school program and includes *Highlights for Children* magazine as a home-school connection material, storybook reading, recording "very own words" from the environment, writing journals, and engaging in storytelling. Parent meetings are held regularly with the children to help them learn to work together using the program strategies that are also used in school. A mentoring program with a small group of parents focuses more closely on the development of their literacy skills. The program takes place in an inner-city school district consisting of African-American and Latino families. The children are in kindergarten through third grades.

Program Success ❖ Parents and children report that they are working together as they never did before. Parents report that the nature of the activities used in the program is fun, including storytelling, collecting very own words, and using the *Highlights for Children Magazine.* Parents enjoy the activities as much as their children, and that is one of the reasons they participate. Teachers report increased interest and achievement in reading and writing from children whose parents participate.

Reference
Morrow, L.M., et al. (1995). The Family WRAP Program: Writing and Reading Appreciation Program for Parents and Pupils. In L.M. Morrow (Ed.),

Family literacy connections in schools and communities. Newark, DE: International Reading Association.

The Home English Literacy for Parents Project (HELP)
Chicago, Illinois

Program Description ❖ The Home English Literacy for Parents Project (HELP) is implemented in school programs in the northwest Chicago area. Parents attend school for 5 hours a week at seven school sites. HELP integrates practical knowledge with literacy and parenting skills and is divided into two phases. Phase I focuses on everyday survival competencies such as reading a bill or writing a check. Phase II focuses on school competencies such as understanding a child's report card or writing a note to the teacher and also includes parenting lessons that correspond with each literacy activity. The activities give the parents an opportunity to model literacy behaviors and learn skills that support a child's academic life.

Success ❖ Because of the integration of literacy skills with survival competencies, adults have a keen motivation to stay with the program. Children have been positively affected by their parents' new ability to become involved in their education.

Reference
Terdy, D., & Berkovitz, L. (1989). *Home English literacy for parents: An ESL literacy curriculum.* (ERIC Document Reproduction Service No. ED 313 926)

Houston Read Commission
Houston, Texas

Program Description ❖ The Houston READ Commission was established by the Houston City Council in 1988 to address the needs of the poor in a city where over half a million adults lack basic literacy skills. Fourteen neighborhood literacy centers were established with the support of both public and private sectors. Each center has a local sponsor who helps staff and equip the center and helps underwrite a student assistance fund that provides emergency assistance, transportation, and babysitting services. The centers are open for 50 hours a week and offer various parallel programs for parents and children ranging in age from preschool to high school. As children receive preschool and homework instruction, their parents take courses in basic skills, parenting, life skills, and employment training.

In 1989, the Houston READ Commission began to sponsor a Reading Is Fundamental (RIF) program at 12 of its neighborhood literacy centers, which serve 4,400 youngsters and their parents. RIF enhances each center's efforts to involve adult learners in their children's reading efforts. Each center has its own Houston READ staff, volunteers, and a RIF council, which is made up of adult learner parents. Parents make all the important decisions about the program, such as deciding which books to purchase for RIF distributions and which themes to use. They provide refreshments, decorate the centers, and hold fund-raising activities to raise money for books. Volunteers come from all walks of life, and include high-risk teenagers recruited through the Houston Job Training Partnership Program who were trained to work in the summer as tutors, homework coaches, and RIF volunteers. This involvement helped motivate these teenagers to stay in school. Neighborhood centers interact among one another in reading competitions and share author visits and book reading clubs. One of the Houston READ Commission's literacy centers, Star of Hope, also serves as a transitional living center for single mothers and their children. Through the joint efforts of Houston READ, RIF, and Houston IRA, these mothers have the opportunity to develop both their own and their children's literacy skills.

Program Success ❖ Parents in the program have developed an enthusiasm for reading that is passed down to their children. Involvement in running the program promotes confidence and self-esteem. At-risk teen volunteers have been motivated to remain in school.

Reference
Reading Is Fundamental. (1991). Houston READ Commission. In *A guide to RIF's family literacy programs* (pp. 37–38). Washington, DC: Author.

Intergenerational Literacy Project
Boston, Massachusetts

Program Description ❖ This program is implemented in Chelsea, Massachusetts, a multicultural community. Parents attend literacy classes 4 days per week, 2 hours per day, over a 15-week instructional cycle. At the same time, their preschoolers are provided with free child care. The adult classes focus on basic instruction in reading skills and family contexts for literacy use, especially storybook reading. Also, parents are encouraged to build a portfolio of their children's uses of literacy at home. Elementary school teachers have been provided with the names of children whose families participate in this program and are encouraged to invite parents to share with them their project experiences and children's portfolios.

Program Success ❖ The average retention rate over a 3-year period was 74 percent. Pre- and post-program testing of a sample of nine adult participants who began with low print literacy in English revealed improved reading performances (an average decrease in oral reading miscues of 13 percent after 40 instructional hours). An analysis of family literacy behaviors, based on a weekly self-report submitted by 10 families, shows an increase in family literacy activities. These families reported no shared print activities and no library visits prior to program participation. By the last week in the program, however, these families reported reading to children 3 to 4 times per week and having visited a library at least once.

Implications for Teaching: The idea of encouraging parents to keep and share a portfolio of literacy activities at home could be useful and enriching. This practice could also encourage interactive literacy activities at home.

Reference
Paratore, J.R. (In press). Parents and children sharing literacy. In D. Lancey (Ed.), *Emergent literacy: From research to practice.* New York: Praeger.

The Kenan Trust Family Literacy Project
Louisville, KY

Program Description ❖ The Kenan Trust Family Literacy Project was designed to help break the cycle of poverty and illiteracy in families with low literacy levels. This community-based program is in operation at seven sites in Kentucky and North Carolina and lasts for a period of 18 months. The Kenan model strives to improve parents' basic skills and attitudes toward education as well as to improve their children's ability to learn. Participating adults are either the parent or primary caregiver of 3- or 4-year-old children. Public service announcements as well as pamphlets placed in public places have been used to recruit participants. Ninety-five percent of the program's participants are unemployed and receive some form of government assistance.

Parents and children are picked up by a school bus three times a week to attend classes, which are most often held at a local elementary school from 8:30 a.m. to 2:30 p.m. Three staff members, including an early childhood education teacher and an aide, as well as volunteers, work with parents in each program. A typical day at one of the Kenan Trust Family Literacy sites is as follows: (1) 8:45 a.m. to 10:45 a.m., parents receive basic skills instruction or employment preparation training; (2) 10:45 a.m. to 11:00 a.m., parents break; (3) 11:00 a.m. to 11:45 a.m., parents join children for learning activities; (4) 11:45 a.m. to 12:15 p.m., parents and children have lunch together; (5) 1:00 p.m. to 2:30 p.m., parents have a large group discussion centered on parenting skills.

Program Success ❖ The Kenan model successfully instills positive attitudes toward education. The program has a 90 percent retention rate. Some of the parents have been hired to work in the schools after completing the program. Parents have made great gains in literacy skills as their children progressed in their learning development.

Reference

McIvor, M.C. (Ed.). (1990). The Kenan Trust Family Literacy Model. In *Family literacy in action: A survey of successful programs* (pp. 33–37). Syracuse, NY: New Readers Press.

Learning, Earning, and Parenting (LEAP)
Cleveland, Ohio

Program Description ❖ The Cleveland Public School system developed a family literacy program to address the needs of both children and parents and to attempt to break the cycle of illiteracy. In this pilot study, the participants included 50 parents who were eligible under the Job Training Partnership Act (JTPA). They had not graduated from high school and were under 21 years of age for the duration of the project. They attended one of four 9-week sessions (12 hours per week) that ran from September 1989 to June 1990. Their children were aged 2 and under.

The program provided literacy training, pre-employment and job-search activities, and classes on child development and parenting skills. In addition, on-site preschool instruction in kindergarten-readiness was offered to the participants' children.

Program Success ❖ All of the 41 parents who participated for the full duration of the program showed a gain of at least one grade level in their reading skills. All enrolled in a high school completion program and demonstrated a significant increase in knowledge about child development and parent interaction. Twenty-five percent of the children showed some growth in developmental skills. A continuation of the program and a second project are planned.

Reference

A family literacy project, final report. (1990). Cleveland Public Schools, Office of Adult and Continuing Education. (ERIC Document Reproduction Service No. ED 335 5550)

Literacy Broadcast Project
Salinas, California

Program Description ❖ In 1986, the California Human Development Corporation, a nonprofit agency, bought a bilingual radio station,

KHDC-FM, which was meant to serve as an important community resource for the people of Salinas Valley, California. In 1988, Reading Is Fundamental (RIF), engaged KHDC in a joint venture that became the Literacy Broadcast Project. Designed to reach a largely migrant Hispanic population of 133,000, this program's primary goals were the following: to nurture the desire to read; to improve reading skills, and to enhance self-esteem in low-literacy Spanish-speaking families. Broadcasts had an intergenerational approach and featured reading aloud, storytelling, discussions on literacy issues, local history, and shared cultural experiences. Altogether, KHDC developed, produced, and aired 296 programs, involving 800 school children directly in such program activities as reading aloud and dramatic dialogues.

Individual programs included "Roadway to Success," which set out to help illiterate individuals overcome their fears and take concrete steps toward becoming literate. "Raises" featured family storytelling, and "Popolite/Kite" was designed as a storytime program for Spanish-speaking preschoolers. As part of its community outreach, the Literacy Broadcast Project held a two-day book writing workshop for local Girl Scouts and free book distribution at the annual Kid's Day fair at a local mall.

Program Success ❖ The Literacy Broadcast Project successfully supported the schools and libraries of Monterey County, presenting their "human side" to the migrants. The program was also awarded a grant from the California State Department of Education during the 1989–1990 school year.

Reference

Reading Is Fundamental. (1991). Literacy Broadcast Project. In *A guide to RIF's family literacy programs* (pp. 64–68). Washington, DC: Author.

Love, Laps and Learning to Read: A Reading Buddy Program Arizona

Program Description ❖ Love, Laps and Learning to Read is an intergenerational family literacy program dedicated to teaching high school students (especially teen mothers and fathers) about the critical role they play as their children's first teachers. The goals of the program are to introduce high school students to the genre of children's books, to teach them fluent and expressive oral reading techniques that enhance storybook reading for both child and teen, and, to establish for teen parents the connection between early family literacy activities and school success.

The program varies across school districts as determined by local needs and resources. Generally, a 2- or 3-week unit format is followed with daily, specific learning activities. Teens are introduced to familiar children's books; asked to reflect on their own personal memories of favorite books; provided with models of fluent, expressive oral reading through demonstrations and videotapes; and given practice in improving their oral fluency skills. The unit includes the planning of a field trip to an elementary school where each teen meets a reading buddy from a primary grade classroom and reads a story to his or her new reading buddy. Teens work in pairs to develop a plan for their story reading sessions ahead of time.

Program Success ❖ Oral and written comments about the program show observable, positive changes in the attitudes of high school students toward reading. Both high school and elementary classes involved in the program reported nearly perfect attendance on reading buddy days. Homework assigned to teens during the unit was almost always completed once the teens discovered they could not read to their buddies unless their lesson plans were complete. Teens began to bring children's books to school and share them with classmates. Finally, teens often asked to order books from book clubs, just as their primary reading buddies did.

Reference
A complete description of one school's version of a reading buddy program can be found in Enz, B.J., & Searfoss, L.W. (1995). Let the circle be

unbroken: Teens as literacy learners and teachers. In L.M. Morrow (Ed.), *Family literacy connections in schools and communities.* Newark, DE: International Reading Association.

Marin County Library Family Literacy Program
Marin County, California

Program Description ❖ This community-based program is affiliated with both Laubach Literacy Action (LLA) and Literacy Volunteers of America (LVA) and primarily serves Hispanic workers living on ten remote dairy ranches in western Marin County, California. This community is tight-knit, despite the distance between farms. Most of the families immigrated from Jalisco, Mexico. The 75 participants have lived in the United States for 3 to 10 years.

Although this program began as an effort focused exclusively on adult literacy, an intergenerational component was added after 3 years to meet the needs of the farm workers' children. Literacy volunteers tutor both parents and children in their homes for at least 1 1/2 hours per week. Tutors teach parents how to read to their children and introduce new books. They also cover such issues as communication with the child's school. A Hispanic adult learner was hired on a part-time basis to serve as a liaison between the school and the Hispanic community. This person acts as an interpreter in classrooms without a bilingual teacher and helps to plan parent-school activities. Bilingual reading material was purchased for parents to use with their children in the home. Bilingual story times were scheduled at a local library. Once-a-month bookmobile stops, which also offer story readings, were made available at five of the dairy ranches. The bookmobile is stocked with 3,000 books and is staffed by a bilingual literacy volunteer. This program also offers Spanish lessons for Anglo parents at the local schools, bilingual math workshops for both parents and children, and workshops designed to help parents create a "work space" for their children.

Program Success ❖ This program has been extremely successful in recruiting parental involvement. There has been a marked increase in parental participation in school activities. The program has helped

Hispanic children realize that they indeed have a place in their school.

Reference

McIvor, M.C. (Ed.) (1990). Marin County Library Family Literacy Program. In *Family literacy in action: A survey of successful programs* (pp. 7–10). Syracuse, NY: New Readers Press.

Motheread, Inc.
Raleigh, North Carolina

Program Description ❖ Motheread, Inc. is a private, nonprofit organization founded in 1987 that strives to teach adults how to become "reading models" for their children. Motheread operates intergenerational literacy programs for women who are incarcerated in two Raleigh, North Carolina, prisons as well as library-sponsored classes in rural North Carolina and both rural and urban community programs. Reading is taught not only as a skill but also as a means of self-expression and of sharing mutual experiences. The Motheread model was designed to respond to one of the three most often cited reasons for adult enrollment in remedial reading programs: the desire to read to their children. The program's volunteers also teach child care personnel storytelling techniques and provide story-sharing hours in community childcare centers.

Motheread tends to recruit parents who read below the ninth-grade level. It helps prisoners to "reconnect" with their children and stresses the benefit that children will obtain from parental participation in reading activities. Classes are taught by two staff members and two volunteers at the two Raleigh prisons. In the rural and urban community programs, instruction is provided by volunteers. Classes meet twice a week, and each session lasts two hours. The basic curriculum runs for three 8-week sessions. After completing this 6-month cycle, participants may enroll in an independent lab class.

In each session, the teacher introduces a children's book and integrates one specific critical thinking or comprehension skill into the reading activity. The featured book and read-aloud demonstration provide the basis for a group discussion. The book also becomes a vehicle for the exchange of ideas concerning relevant child development issues and personal experiences. Students gradually learn to use language experience and process writing techniques to write stories for themselves and for their children. Motheread also ensures that books are available to the inmates for use during their children's visits.

Program Success ❖ Motheread reports a retention rate of 90 percent in the eight-week sessions and a 60 percent retention rate in the independent lab classes. The staff has reported profound positive changes in students' self-esteem, reading behaviors, and self-perception as parents. The program has also been a catalyst to enrollment in vocational training programs, GED, and high school completion.

Reference

McIvor, M.C. (Ed.) (1990). Motheread, Inc. In *Family literacy in action: A survey of successful programs* (pp. 22–27). Syracuse, NY: New Readers Press.

Mothers' Reading Program
New York, NY

Program Description ❖ The Mothers' Reading Program was designed for mothers of children attending Head Start programs on the lower east side of Manhattan. About 75 women per year participate. This program began in 1985 and is one of several model intergenerational programs designed and implemented by the American Reading Council in New York City. Many of the women enrolled come from Hispanic, African American, Vietnamese, and other ethnic minorities. Their reading levels range from first to third grade. Mothers usually find out about the program through the Head Start Centers or by word-of-mouth. The program takes place at the University Settlement House, which also houses a Head Start program. Many of the participants' children attend Head Start either here or nearby. Classes are held throughout the school year. Mothers attend classes either

Tuesday, Wednesday, and Friday mornings for three hours or for two afternoons per week. The program is based on the philosophy that the context of the learner's immediate environment should be directly linked to the learning experience. Skills are developed through active participation in a group setting. As learning materials, this program uses the "literature" created in the women's writing group. These stories reflect issues and concerns relevant to everyone in the class.

Some class time each year also focuses specifically on the importance of reading as an interaction between parents and children. Mothers and their children take trips to the local public library. Participants are encouraged to borrow books from the program's library, which is run by women in the program who have learned library skills with the help of the American Reading Council. To help mothers realize their immediate language strengths as they learn English, a "whole process approach" is used. The students compose a fictional story through collective dialogue which the teacher writes on the board and the students copy. This is followed by individual work with the teacher on basic grammar and usage.

Program Success ❖ Participants' reading abilities improve by at least two grade levels per year. The instructors report a sense of empowerment in their students. Most of the women stay with the program two or three years before testing out at a fifth-grade reading level. Several of the program's graduates stay on to work with the teachers as program mentors.

Reference

McIvor, M.C. (Ed.) (1990). Mothers' Reading Program. In *Family literacy in action: A survey of successful programs* (pp. 38–42). Syracuse, NY: New Readers Press.

Parent and Child Education Program (PACE)
Kentucky

Program Description ❖ The Parent and Child Education Program (PACE) was started by two Kentucky educators and is administered by the Kentucky Department of Education. The program is offered in 18 classrooms in 12 Kentucky school districts, all but 3 of which offer space in their own school buildings. Parents and children are involved both separately and together in emergent literacy activities. Children attend on-site preschool while parents attend basic skills and parenting classes. Parents are encouraged to serve as educational role models. The families involved in PACE come from a variety of ethnic backgrounds, but all share the feature of low literacy skills.

The program's goals include having all parents obtain a high school equivalency certificate, improve basic skills, and improve parenting skills. The parents' curriculum is based on individual need, and the courses are taught by an adult education teacher. Children are taught by an early childhood teacher, who uses material from a nationally validated, cognitively oriented early childhood curriculum.

Program Success ❖ PACE was one of the 10 winners (out of 970 applicants) of the Innovations Prize, given by the Ford Foundation and Harvard University's John F. Kennedy School of Government. Seventy percent of the adult participants either received a GED or raised their reading level by at least two years as measured by a standardized test. PACE preschoolers have exhibited measurable gains as reported by classroom teachers.

Reference
The Barbara Bush Foundation for Family Literacy. (1989). Parent and Child Education Program (PACE). In *First teachers* (pp. 6–8). Washington, DC: Author.

Parent Readers Program
New York

Program Description ❖ The Parent Readers Program uses adults' motivation for their children's educational development in the service of their own literacy development. The Program provides adults with the tools to be reading resources for their children. A key idea underlying the approach is that providing enjoyable and instructive experiences with quality children's books will foster the literacy development of adults and help them foster the literacy development of their children.

Ongoing since 1987, the Parent Readers Program is a voluntary workshop series at New York City Technical College of the City University of New York that consists of three workshops, followed by a family reading celebration. Organized around a theme, each workshop introduces adult participants to children's books of a variety of genres with an accompanying reading and discussion strategy. A linked adult reading provides opportunities for further strategy application and additional discussion.

The components of the model produce both literacy and social outcomes. Introductory activities include reading memories and then at subsequent workshops reporting on the reading at home. The next components include introduction of the genre and book, introduction and modeling of the strategy, paired reading, discussion, preparation for the reading at home, and book borrowing.

A family reading celebration on a Saturday at the end of the program provides an occasion for children and adults to enjoy storytelling, singing, and reading together.

Outcomes include the following:

- Participants' reading improves as they apply the reading strategies to their own reading.
- Adults involve children in reading activities and teach children reading behaviors and attitudes learned in the workshops.
- Adults become sensitive to factors that can affect a reading relationship with a child, such as pinpointing his or her interests, disposition, and developmental needs.
- Adults serve as reading role models.

- Adults become literacy resources by providing more opportunities for reading, such as encouraging library visits, bringing books home, and reading to neighborhood children.

Program Success ❖ The Parent Readers Program was featured in *First Teachers*, published by the Barbara Bush Foundation for Family Literacy, and in *Family Literacy in Action: A Survey of Successful Programs*, published by New Readers Press. The program is one of three described in the first family literacy documentary, produced as part of the Lifelong Learning Project by WQED with funding from the U.S. Department of Education. In 1993, the Parent Readers Program won the national Excellence in English Award from the English-Speaking Union.

References

Handel, R.D., & Goldsmith, E. (1994). Family reading: Still got it: Adults as learners, literacy resources, and actors in the world, In D. Dickinson (Ed.), *Bridges to Literacy: Approaches to Supporting Child and Family Literacy* (pp. 150–174). Cambridge, MA: Blackwell, Inc.

Handel, R.D., & Goldsmith, E. (1988). "Intergenerational literacy: A community college program," *Journal of Reading*, 250–256.

For further information, contact Ellen Goldsmith, Director, Center for Intergenerational Reading, New York City Technical College, 300 Jay Street, Brooklyn, New York 11201.

Parents and Children Together
Nationwide

Program Description ❖ Parents and Children Together is a nationwide literacy program established by the National Center for Family Literacy (NCFL) in Louisville, Kentucky. Parents who lack a high school diploma and their 3- and 4-year old children attend school together between 3 and 5 days a week. This varies depending on the site. High quality early childhood education is provided for the children, while the parents attend an adult education program to learn reading, math, and parenting skills. The program's early childhood education component develops children's verbal skills, increasing their vocabulary and encouraging them to talk. They are also taught reading-readiness skills such as identifying colors and shapes, as well as social skills such as sharing.

Many parents in the program enter with the hope of passing the high school equivalency exam and thereby bettering themselves for the benefit of their children. The adults are encouraged to think critically and creatively, regardless of their backgrounds and abilities. In addition to improving their reading and math skills, parents are taught to set goals and collaborate with their peers in the program's second component. "Parent Time" is the program's third component, during which the adults discuss a variety of topics ranging from discipline to self-esteem. Instructors provide information about advocacy programs, and parents reach out to one another in mutual support and friendship.

The program's fourth component is "Parent and Child Together" time (PACT). During this hour, families play together. The activities are led by the children. Parents find that they can learn both with and from their children. The early childhood teaching strategies used by the instructors are taught to the parents.

Program Success ❖ A 1991 study of children who had completed this NCFL family literacy program showed that not one of them had repeated a grade in elementary school. Without this program, one-quarter of these at-risk children would have been retained by the time they reached the fourth grade. Seventy-five percent of the participant children were found to be performing at or above average, and 42 percent were rated in the top third of their class. Many parents have succeeded in obtaining GEDs.

Reference

The National Center for Family Literacy. (1993). Parents and Children Together. In *Creating an upward spiral of success* (pp. 6–8). Louisville, KY: Author.

Parents as Partners in Reading: A Family Literacy Training Program
National

Program Description ❖ Dr. Patricia A. Edwards developed the Parents as Partners in Reading (PAPIR) program in Donaldsonville, Louisiana, while she was an assistant professor at Louisiana State University. She is now a Professor of Language and Literacy and a Senior Researcher at the National Center for Teacher Learning at Michigan State University. The program seeks to improve the literacy rate among socioeconomically deprived families by teaching parents how to read to their children—something that does not come naturally to those who are not brought up in environments that promote literacy. Soon after PAPIR was implemented in schools, libraries, and community centers, educators began asking Edwards to expand it (which resulted in the development of *Talking Your Way to Literacy: A Program to Help Nonreading Parents Prepare their Children for Reading*). This program was developed with one thing in mind: to emphasize the fact that illiterate parents can use their knowledge and experience to help their children learn to read. The program lessons blend oral language experiences of families with conventional language uses in the classroom.

Program Success ❖ PAPIR was one of five early childhood programs highlighted on the WQED/ABC Project Literacy U.S. documentary "First Things First" and one of 10 family literacy programs highlighted by the Barbara Bush Foundation for Family Literacy. The programs also received commendation in the national press. Since the publication of the two programs, educators from 44 out of the 50 states have used the programs with great success. The programs are now available in Spanish. The overwhelming result of those who have used these materials is that both parents and children have exhibited measurable gains.

Reference
Edwards, P.A. (1993). *Parents as Partners in Reading: A Family Training Program*. Second Edition. Chicago, IL: Childrens Press.

The Partnership for Family Reading
New Jersey: Montclair State College

Program Description ❖ The Partnership for Family Reading, operating in 34 schools in a New Jersey urban district, provides workshops for families with children in kindergarten through grade 3. The Partnership uses the Family Reading model—workshops in which adult family members experience the pleasure of children's books and learn how to use active reading and discussion strategies when reading with children at home. Quality, multicultural books in English and Spanish are provided. Teachers receive intensive staff development in the workshop model and the literature-based curriculum units.

The aims of the program are to motivate and equip adults to serve as literacy resources for their children; to foster the literacy development of all family members; and to help teachers take on the role of family literacy educator.

Program Success ❖ Parents have fostered the literacy development of their children, developed their own learning skills, and built reading relationships within the family, school, and community. Children have shown increases in motivation and knowledge of books and reading strategies. Teachers have established productive ways of working with adult family members and have adapted Family Reading methodology to classroom instruction.

Nationally, over 200 additional schools have adopted the program. The model was cited by the Barbara Bush Foundation as one of ten "pioneering and promising" family literacy programs.

Reference
Handel, R.D. (1992). The Partnership for Family Reading: Benefits for Families and Schools. *The Reading Teacher, 46* 116–126.

Contact: Ruth D. Handel, Director, Partnership for Family Reading, Montclair State University, Upper Montclair, New Jersey 07043.

Project Flame: A Literacy Program for Language Minority Families
Illinois

Program Description ❖ Project FLAME (Family Literacy: Aprendiendo, Mejorando, Educando [Learning, Bettering, Educating]) provides literacy training and support to Latino parents who are not yet proficient in English. FLAME is operated by the University of Illinois at Chicago's Center for Literacy in 8 Chicago Public Schools. Families must have a child between the ages of 3 and 9 in order to enroll. Parents attend twice weekly ESL/Basic Skills classes to work on their own language and literacy development. Twice monthly they attend "Parents as Teachers" classes, where they learn to help their children to learn literacy. These classes emphasize selecting and sharing books, using the library, teaching letters and sounds, improving writing and math skills, helping with homework, and other topics. No direct instruction of children is provided by the program (this is done by the parents themselves). The Parents as Teachers sessions are now taught by parents who have completed the program successfully.

FLAME shows parents how to provide a home environment that is supportive of their children's literacy development. It teaches them how this can be accomplished in ways that are consistent with the social and cultural contexts of the family. The parents' own successful language and literacy learning in the program is an essential component of helping their children to succeed in school.

Program Success ❖ More than 300 families have now completed the FLAME program since 1989. As a result of participation, parents improved their English language proficiency as measured by standardized tests and qualitative indicators. Some have used these skills to get jobs, enroll in community colleges, or get elected to Local School Councils. Preschool children improved significantly on several school readiness instruments and showed greater improvement than nonparticipants. In school, FLAME children were less likely to be retained or to need special educational services. Parent involvement in their children's education increased.

References

For more information see Shanahan, T., Mulhern, M., & Rodriguez-Brown. (1995). Project FLAME: Lessons Learned from a Family Literacy Program for Linguistic Minority Students. *The Reading Teacher, 47* (7). Or contact Timothy Shanahan, UIC Center for Literacy, 1040 W. Harrison (M/C 147), Chicago, IL 60607.

Project Pact (Parent and Child Together)
Laurinburg, North Carolina

Program Description ❖ This literacy program was conducted by the Scotland County Memorial Library in Laurinburg, North Carolina. The program trained two tutors and two volunteers in the storybook method of teaching reading. A public awareness campaign was directed to recruit adults who wanted to learn to read to their children and grandchildren. A one-on-one tutoring approach was used. It had a two-fold purpose: to improve participants' own reading skills while also teaching them how to read to children. A computer was purchased and proved popular with low-literacy adults. At the same time, participant children attended story hour and received school-readiness lessons. At the end of the session, adults and children came together to share a book.

Program Success ❖ During the year-long programs, the 10 parents reported that they liked the reading approach. Some who did not know how to read before were now able to read for the first time.

Reference

Bush, P.A. (1989). *Project Pact (Parent and Child Together). Final performance report.* (ERIC Document Reproduction Service No. ED 333 125)

Project WILL (Women in Laubach Literacy)
Pine Bluff, Arkansas

Program Description ❖ This intergenerational volunteer literacy program was founded in 1986 by the Literacy Council of Jefferson County, Arkansas. It offers one-on-one reading instruction to women with low-level literacy skills while providing free child care in the project's day-care facility. Special literacy development activities are provided for the children. Free transportation is provided, and there is no limit to how long a woman may participate. Children may continue until age 12. Classes are held on the campus of the University of Arkansas at Pine Bluff. Tutors and students were initially recruited through such means as public service announcements. Many university students majoring in education serve as volunteers.

Project WILL is an ongoing program and breaks only for Thanksgiving, Christmas, and a 3-week summer holiday. Students are tutored twice a week for an hour each session. All the women also attend two 1-hour group activities or discussion sessions each week. Issues include the following: family life enrichment, safety issues, personal growth, and educational motivation. The program uses phonics-based curriculum designed to bring students up to a fifth-grade reading level as well as supplemental lesson material including high-interest/low level fiction and nonfiction and crossword puzzles. Books, including children's literature, may be checked out at the library conference room.

While the mothers participate in their tutoring and group sessions, their children are offered many learning experiences, including verbal development activities, singing, and coloring. Once every 6 weeks, a mother in the program visits the day-care facility and reads a book to the children. The project coordinator teaches mothers about the importance of reading to children and how to enhance a child's listening skills.

Program Success ❖ Because each woman enters the program with unique objectives, results vary. There are usually 35 women in the program, about half of whom are mothers. Some go on to receive their GED. Students are tested every 6 months using the WRAT. There is a 65 to 70 percent retention rate. Program staff have reported that the women enjoy coming to a college campus and are convinced that Project WILL meets a real need in their community.

Reference

McIvor, M.C. (Ed.) (1990). Project WILL. In *Family literacy in action: A survey of successful programs* (pp. 28–32). Syracuse, NY: New Readers Press.

Reading Starts With Us
New York

Program Description ❖ Reading Starts With Us has three interrelated aims:

- to train day care and Head Start staff to foster family literacy,
- to motivate and equip parents to read to children at home, thereby positioning adults to use reading relationships to enhance their children's literacy development, and
- to promote meaningful partnerships between parents and teachers.

Reading Starts With Us uses the Family Reading model—a series of workshops in which adult family members experience the pleasure of quality children's books and learn active reading and discussion strategies to use at home and with their children.

Reading Starts With Us is a two-part program. In the first stage, teams of day care and Head Start teachers receive five experiential training workshops. In the second stage, teacher teams provide four on-site workshops for parents of the children in their classes. Two features of the workshops are key. First, they are experiential. Participants experience children's literature so they can then recreate the quality of those experiences at home. Second, they are social. Discussion, sharing, and discovery are central. The mode of communication is not lecture, and there are no right and wrong answers. Ongoing technical assistance—consisting of at least one site visit for each agency whose staff received training and ongoing seminars and meetings throughout the year—helps teachers to form support groups and to learn from one another.

Program Success ❖ Observations and reports have shown that the following dramatic changes took place in parents, children, and teachers:

- Parents read more frequently to their children and learned about their children's interests and ideas through observation and conversation about the books.
- Parents set up libraries at home and participated in trips to the library.
- Parents learned about their importance as reading role models.
- Children listened more attentively at story time.
- Children gravitated to the book corner more frequently and did more "pretend reading."
- Children told more of their own stories and talked more about books.
- Teachers learned about reading strategies and about the value of reading different types of books.
- Teachers enjoyed parents' appreciation of their efforts and formed closer relationships with parents.
- Teachers felt a sense of satisfaction in playing a role that assured ongoing literacy activities for the children in their classes.

Reading Starts With Us is currently being evaluated using an ethnographic approach.

References

Goldsmith, E. (1993). Translations and transformations: From training to implementation. *Literacy Harvest, 2*(2), 9–16.

Goldsmith, E., & Handel, R.D. (1990). *Family Reading: An Intergenerational Approach to Literacy*. Syracuse, NY: New Readers Press.

For further information, contact Ellen Goldsmith, Director, Center for Intergenerational Reading, New York City Technical College, 300 Jay Street, Brooklyn, New York 11201.

Read Together
Pittsburgh, Pennsylvania

Program Description ❖ Read Together was implemented by Beginning with Books, a nonprofit, early intervention literacy organization affiliated with the Carnegie Library of Pittsburgh. This program provides storybook sessions for children whose parents are concurrently attending the literacy tutoring program. Free transportation is provided. This program began after Beginning with Books surveyed adults enrolled in a literacy tutoring program to find out what had prompted them to seek this kind of help. Many of the responses were linked to the desire to help one's children. The lack of child care was cited as the main reason that had prevented them from enrolling earlier. The Read Together program was designed to meet the needs of such parents. This program recruits and trains volunteers and then matches them on a one-on-one basis with participants. The sessions take place in the children's room of a designated branch library. Children may continue to attend even if the parent discontinues.

At the first session, a staff member introduces all the members of the Read Together team: the parent, the child, the parent's tutor, and the child's tutor. The parent then goes on to his or her own tutoring session. At the same time, the child's tutor and the child become acquainted. The tutor guides him or her through various literacy experiences. Most parents read below the fourth-grade level and may not be confident enough to start reading to their children at home right away. However, they are encouraged to borrow books, book-tape sets, and tape players from the library to use at home.

Program Success ❖ Anecdotal evidence demonstrates that both the parents and children are enthusiastic about the program and about reading. The co-directors have noted that the children have shown impressive emotional and social growth.

Reference

McIvor, M.C. (Ed.). (1990). Beginning with Books—Read Together Program. In *Family literacy in action: A survey of successful programs* (pp. 11–15). Syracuse, NY: New Readers Press.

SER (Service Education and Redevelopment)
Family Learning Centers (FLCs)
of SER-Jobs for Progress, Inc.
Nationwide

Program Description ❖ SER-Jobs for Progress was founded in 1964 as a voluntary community-based organization; it now operates 111 programs in 83 U.S. cities. SER programs are designed to meet the needs of Hispanics in terms of education, training, employment, and economic opportunities. Since 1986, literacy training and basic remedial education became the primary service offered to the participants. SER National has implemented its Hispanic literacy initiative through the Family Learning Center (FLC) concept. These programs are funded by the U.S. Departments of Labor, Education, and Health and Human Services, as well as from private sector contributions.

The FLC provides basic and job skills training, literacy councils, and intergenerational enriched child care, while SER provides literacy training, GED, employment skills, and parenting information. Preschoolers receive social, cultural, and health-related services, in addition to spending one hour per day using educational technology and software. They also are taught prereading and language development activities. Parent literacy training is provided in automated learning environments led by certified teachers. The curriculum includes English as a second language, basic adult education, basic literacy, life-coping skills, health education, and high school equivalency preparation.

Program Success ❖ Many of the adult participants have succeeded in obtaining GEDs. Parents have become more actively involved in their children's education and have become more motivated to continue learning.

Reference

The Barbara Bush Foundation for Family Literacy. (1989). SER Family Learning Centers (FLCs) of SER-Jobs for Progress, Inc. In *First teachers* (pp. 16–18). Washington, DC: Author.

Take Up Reading Now (TURN)
Washington, DC

Program Description ❖ This community-based program was established in 1985 under the auspices of Push Literacy Action Now (PLAN), an organization that has provided reading and writing instruction to low-literacy adults in the Washington, D.C., area since 1972. In this area, two-thirds of all female heads of families are living below the poverty line and are high school dropouts. These women are the parents of 35,000 educationally at-risk children. TURN was established not only to improve these parents' literacy and parenting skills but also to increase their children's chances for success in school.

TURN's outreach efforts involve three distinct programs. Take CARE (Child Advocacy for Reading Education) helps parents become knowledgeable advocates for children who are experiencing difficulties in school. Take a Book is a program that collects and distributes new and good condition used books to low-income families. Take PART (Parents as Reading Teachers) works with parents to show them how they can become their children's first teachers.

TURN regularly conducts workshops at public health clinics, community centers, and public housing complexes. Eighty percent of the 3,000 participants stated in their initial interview that their main objective was to be able to help their children. TURN teaches parents or primary caregivers how children learn and demonstrates new activities in which they can stimulate their children to develop cognitive skills. The program includes a focus on specific reading activities, such as one-hour parent-child reading sessions. A special seven-session program for parents who are unable to attend on a regular basis was also established. The program covers such issues as the importance of parents' participation in children's learning processes, the importance of reading, and how to choose an appropriate children's book.

Program Success ❖ In follow-up conversations with parents, many reported that they enjoy reading activities with their children. As of May 1989, 350 parents have participated in all of the TURN programs.

Reference

McIvor, M.C. (1990). Take Up Reading Now (TURN). In *Family literacy in action: A survey of successful programs* (pp. 43–47). Washington, DC: Reading Is Fundamental.

Toyota Families for Learning Program
Nationwide

Program Description ❖ This program was funded through grants from the Toyota Motor Corporation made to the National Center for Family Literacy in Kentucky. Toyota Families for Learning helps undereducated parents increase their literacy and life skills as their children attend preschool under the same roof. Parents and children develop a learning partnership. Programs have been established in 15 cities selected through an application process that is based on three things: (1) the level of need indicated by poverty and low adult literacy levels, (2) documented commitment of education and government officials, and (3) the plan for collaboration with related programs and resources.

The Toyota program has four integrated components: early childhood education, adult education, parent time, and parent and child time (PACT). During part of the program day, children are taught to improve verbal, reading-readiness, and social skills. Parents are taught basics literacy and math skills. They also learn to set goals, collaborate with peers, and reach out for mutual support. During "parent time," parents discuss a variety of topics ranging from discipline to self-esteem. Teachers inform parents about advocacy programs available to them. During the PACT hour, families come together for various intergenerational learning activities. Many parents realize for the first time that they can teach their children. After sharing a lunch time, children nap as parents volunteer in the school.

Program Success ❖ At the beginning of the program, 93 percent of the children scored at or below the 25th percentile nationwide in the Peabody Picture Vocabulary Test. Over half scored in the bottom 1 percent of all American children. After completing the program year, 27 percent of the children who had scored in the bottom quarter were now above the 25th percentile and no longer in the "at risk" category. Nearly 60 percent of those in the bottom 1 percent increased their scores, and the percentage of children scoring at or above average increased dramatically.

Reference

The National Center for Family Literacy. (no year). Toyota Families for Learning Program. In *Creating an upward spiral of success* (pp. 11–18) (pamphlet). Louisville, KY: Author.

The Weber State University/Standard Examiner
Family Literacy Project
Ogden, Utah

Program Description ❖ This community-based program is designed to improve low-literacy skills of parents while developing the preliteracy abilities of their children. The program lasts for 5 months and offers preparation classes for the GED and parent and child together (PACT) time. The preschool classes have a curriculum that focuses on cognitive development, the whole child, and free choice of activities for the children. After the parents attend a GED preparation class and the children attend their preschool program, they come together for PACT time. PACT time is meant to improve the communication skills of both the child and the adult and to help the parents value positive interaction with their own children. During PACT time, parents and children play together, with the children taking the lead.

Program Success ❖ The parents involved in the program showed positive changes in the areas of personal growth and self-esteem. Attitudes toward education improved.

Reference

Glover, R.J. et al. (1991). Family literacy: A formative evaluation of program outcomes. *Contemporary education, 62*(4), pp. 324–326.

Research on Naturally Occurring Literacy in Families

RESEARCH ON NATURALLY OCCURRING LITERACY IN-
VOLVES OBSERVING AND DESCRIBING LITERACY EVENTS
THAT TAKE PLACE IN THE ROUTINE OF FAMILIES' DAILY
LIVES. THIS RESEARCH OFTEN DOES NOT HAVE A DELIB-
ERATE CONNECTION WITH THE SCHOOL CURRICULUM BUT
FOCUSES ON HOW FAMILIES USE LITERACY NATURALLY
WITHIN THEIR HOMES.

Anderson, B., & Stokes, S.J. (1984). Social and institutional influences on the development and practice of literacy. In H. Goelman, A.A. Oberg, & F. Smith (Eds.), *Awakening to literacy* (pp. 24–37). Portsmouth, NH: Heinemann.

Purpose of the Study ❖ To challenge the assumptions that books provide the only valuable literacy experiences for preschoolers and that ethnic or cultural factors mitigate against literacy practice and development.

Procedures ❖ Observations focused on preschool children and were made during home visits of three equally represented ethnic groups in San Diego, CA—Anglo Americans, African Americans, and Mexican Americans—over a period of 18 months. A total of 2,000 hours (covering 91 hours per child) of observation took place. Field notes and detailed categorizations of specific literacy events were used.

Results ❖ All families came into contact with print. The frequency and duration of the preschoolers' experiences with print were determined largely by parents and other literate individuals. Although Anglo American parents initiated the greatest number of individual events that communicated the importance of literacy, African American and Mexican American parents spent more time participating in a given event with their children. African Americans were more likely to wait for children to initiate literacy activities.

Implications for Teaching ❖ The planning of child-initiated family literacy events as an appropriate approach in some cultures should be considered and implemented.

Auerbach, E.B. (1989). Toward a social-contextual approach to family literacy. *Harvard Educational Review, 59*(2), 165–181.

Purpose of the Study ❖ To develop an alternative framework to family literacy program design (not based on the "deficit model") that focuses on family strengths, and in which community concerns and cultural practices inform curriculum development.

Procedures ❖ Staff members of the University of Massachusetts/ Boston English Family Literacy Project developed their own conceptual framework by examining current models for family literacy programs, ethnographic literature on family contributions to literacy, and evidence provided by the program's own students. Project staff "listened, read, and talked with students about literacy in their lives."

Results ❖ A gap was found between research and implementation. Existing family literacy program models did not appear to be informed by ethnographic research or substantiated by information provided by the English Family Literacy Project's students.

Implications for Teaching ❖ Local community concerns and cultural practices should be considered in curriculum development. Teachers need to have an open-minded view toward what may be defined as literacy practice in cultures different from their own.

Baghban, M. (1994). Sisters and brothers reading together: An untapped resource in family literacy. Queens College, City University of New York, Department of Elementary and Early Childhood Education and Services (on-going project).

Purpose of the Study ❖ To investigate the reading between two siblings, an older sister and younger brother, to note whether their dialogue about books and their behavior in reading interactions parallel parent-child reading.

Procedures ❖ The participants are the investigators' own children, recorded at least three times a week reading together at home over four years. Observations begin when the 8-year-old sister shows the pictures in books to her 3-day old brother and conclude one year after the younger brother reads two books in a row to his sister. Caregiver diaries, tape recordings photographs, and interviews are used.

Results ❖ Interactions between children do not always go smoothly. Often the older sibling refuses to read when the younger sibling asks, selects a book that she would like to read but the younger sibling would not, or shows impatience with the younger sibling. However, when the reading sessions go well, the younger sibling pays rapt attention and learns fast, better than in interactions with adults.

Implications for Teaching ❖ Often parents are working. They juggle time at home doing chores for the family's survival. Children may leave school to go to empty houses. Siblings increasingly have more time with each other than they do with their parents. Parents and teachers can design activities and workshops which include specific ways to foster positive reading experiences between sisters and brothers.

Baker, L., et al. (1993). Context of emergent literacy: Everyday home experiences of urban pre-kindergarten school children. University of Maryland, Department of Psychology (on-going project).

Purpose of the Study ❖ To investigate the contexts in which children from various sociocultural backgrounds experience literacy as they enter school, and how the overlapping contexts of school and home interact to facilitate or impede reading development.

Procedures ❖ Participants consist of 38 children enrolled in pre-kindergarten programs during the 1992–1993 school year in the Baltimore City, Maryland, area. They are from low- and middle-income African American and white families. The researchers will work with the same children and their teachers over a period of 4 years. Caregiver diaries, home and classroom observation, and interviews are used.

Results ❖ At least 85 percents of the parents in each group reported that their children had storybooks read to them at least once a week. Only 36 percent of the low-income parents reported daily book reading, while 88 percent of the middle-income parents did. There were few overall differences among the sociocultural groups in terms of the play activities of the children. Further analysis is forthcoming.

Implications for Teaching ❖ Teachers must attempt to meet the emergent literacy needs of all preschoolers, with a sensitivity to the variation in home backgrounds and exposure to print that characterize the individual experience of each child.

Barton, D. (1989). *Making sense of literacy in the home.* Paper presented at the Conference of the European Association for Research on Learning and Instruction (Madrid, Spain). (ERIC Document Reproduction Service No. ED 325 812)

Purpose of the Study ❖ To examine the role of literacy in people's everyday lives.

Procedures ❖ Twenty individuals between the ages of 20 and 30 who had received minimal formal education (all had dropped out of school between the ages of 15 and 16) and their children were studied. All lived in Lancashire, England. Methods used were detailed interviews (of about 2 hours per subject; some were interviewed more than once); case studies of individual households; and observations of neighborhood uses of literacy.

Results ❖ Barton found that his subjects tended to have a special time and place set aside for writing and had favorite pens and types of paper. The most common types of literacy activities included sending greeting cards and postcards, writing letters, and writing checks for bills. Types of literacy activities were strongly gender related. Women tended to write personal correspondence, while men tended to take care of business correspondence. Children's literacy roles in the family included such activities as getting the mail and being the first to read the newspaper. The prevalent feeling toward reading by the subjects was that it was "better than doing nothing," but not as important as working.

Implications for Teaching ❖ Teachers should learn what types of literacy activities take place in their students' homes and relate the early reading and writing activities of their students to familiar backgrounds and events.

Bissex, G.L. (1984). The child as teacher. In H. Goelman, A.A. Oberg, & F. Smith (Eds.), Awakening to literacy (pp. 87–109). Portsmouth, NH: Heinemann.

Purpose of the study ❖ To examine self-teaching, self-corrective language, and writing strategies of children in the home and classroom environments.

Procedures ❖ Scott, a preschooler from a working-class background, and Paul, a first grader from a middle-class background, were observed using field notes and student portfolio analysis. Scott was lagging behind in literacy skills, while Paul was advanced.

Results ❖ Paul used invented spellings well before he was much of a reader. His quiet home environment fostered learning, and he explored reading and writing on his own. He showed evidence of self-corrective literacy behavior as his invented spelling progressed to conventional spelling. Scott showed evidence of directing his own learning, especially as seen in his student portfolio, and he benefited greatly from the daily hour-long quiet drawing/writing time in the classroom. Bissex concludes that the role of education should be to "affirm each child's inner teacher."

Implications for Teaching ❖ Teachers need to create opportunities for independent, self-directed reading and writing activities in the classroom, even with young children, and should be aware of and work with each child's own sense of self-direction.

Clark, M.M. (1984). Literacy at home and at school: Insights from a study of young fluent readers. In G. Goelman, A.A. Oberg, & F. Smith (Eds.), *Awakening to literacy* (pp. 122–130). Portsmouth, NH: Heinemann.

Purpose of the Study ❖ To collect insights on the home environment and development of children who make rapid progress toward literacy when they enter school.

Procedures ❖ An in-depth study of 5-year-olds (20 boys and 12 girls) who were fluent readers upon entering school. Parents were interviewed first when their children entered school and again 2 years later. Information was obtained on children's school progress for an additional 2 years. Results of conventional reading tests were studied.

Results ❖ These children's homes were characterized as having large quantities of books. Several had professional parents or older siblings who were successful in school. Positive and extended interactions with an adult was a feature of the backgrounds of all of these children. Such interaction did not always involve books or formal reading instruction.

Implications for Teaching ❖ It is important to create a literacy environment in the classroom in which positive experiences create pleasurable associations with reading in various contexts. Teachers need to create opportunities for oral language interactions with young children as a means of preparing them for reading and writing.

Delgado-Gaitan, C. (1992). School matters in the Mexican-American home: Socializing children to education. *American Educational Research Journal, 29*(3), 495–513.

The Purpose of the Study ❖ The purpose of the study was to determine the attitudes of Mexican-American families toward the education of their children and the roles played by these families. A major goal was to observe and describe the physical surroundings—emotional and motivational climates and interpersonal interactions between parent and child.

Procedures ❖ Six working-class Mexican-American families with second graders were studied. Three of the children were in advanced reading classes and three were in novice classes. Parents were interviewed and observed in spontaneous parent-child interactions. Data was collected in the form of field notes, audio tapes, and video tapes.

Results ❖ Results of the study demonstrated that parents provided a safe, comfortable physical environment and special areas for study, in spite of space limitations. All the parents verbally emphasized their desire to have their children succeed in school. Parents called upon relatives, coworkers, and church friends to assist them or their children with school-related matters. Parents punished their children for poor grades and rewarded them for good grades. Parents' attempts to help children with homework sometimes were fruitless because they could not always understand the directions, and sometimes they inadvertently misled the children. All the parents believed strongly that a person cannot be considered well-educated only because of "book learning." They must also learn to be respectful, well-mannered, and helpful to those in need. Interpersonal interactions between parents and children were characterized by an abundance of verbal exchanges, often revolving around school-related activities. Family stories about life in Mexico guided the children's emotional and moral learning. There were no significant differences in attitudes between the parents of advanced and novice readers.

Implications for Practice ❖ It appears that schools need to respond to Latinos' concerns for children learning good manners and respect in the curriculum. The schools need to be aware of language problems that parents encounter and that verbal interaction, such as oral history and storytelling, is an important aspect of the culture.

Eldridge-Hunter, D. (1992). Intergenerational literacy: Impact on the development of the storybook reading behaviors of Hispanic mothers. In C.K. Kinzer, et al. (Eds.), *Literacy research, theory, and practice: Views from many perspectives* (pp. 101–110). Chicago, IL: National Reading Conference, Inc.

Purpose of the Study ❖ To extend research documenting the impact of intergenerational literacy programs on the lives of literacy project participants and to contribute to a body of research in storybook reading experiences.

Procedures ❖ Four subjects audio-taped themselves at home sharing storybooks with their children approximately every 4 to 6 weeks. The database included 16 storybooks for a total of 157: 05 minutes of tape time. Maternal utterances were analyzed and placed in five distinct coding categories: interactions, responses, questions, functions, and focus.

Results ❖ Areas most likely to be affected by specific (program) instruction are maternal responsiveness to child initiations; semantic contingency of maternal responses; and focus of maternal utterances on literacy. None of the subjects adopted totally new behaviors; they modified previous ones.

Implications for Teaching ❖ Sharing knowledge about storybook reading methods with parents can enhance the parent-child experience at home. Conversely, listening to parents describe such experiences can provide new perspectives and ideas for teachers.

Ferdman, B.M. (1990). Literacy and cultural identity. *Harvard Educational Review*, 60(2), 181–201.

Purpose of the Study ❖ To examine how literacy behavior is framed and defined by cultural contexts.

Procedures ❖ By a review of research literature, Ferdman provides a theoretical framework for examining the influence of literacy and culture on the individual.

Results ❖ Ferdman arrives at a definition of literacy as "facility in manipulating the symbols that codify and represent the values, beliefs, and norms" of a given culture. The goal of literacy acquisition for all can only be achieved through a better understanding of the connection between literacy and culture.

Implications for Teaching ❖ Teachers must be educated as to the meaning and use of literacy in the ethnic backgrounds of their students in order to enrich their teaching style and curriculum with material of relevance and interest to all.

Heath, S.B. (1986). Separating "things of the imagination" from life: Learning to read and write. In W.H. Teale & E. Sulzby (Eds.), *Emergent literacy* (pp. 156–172). Norwood, NJ: Ablex Publishing.

Purpose of the Study ❖ To "pull apart the linguistic features characterizing the activities provided in each kind of home" in order to discover how children learn the habits that make them good or poor readers and writers and contribute to overall success in school.

Procedures ❖ Three communities were studied: Trackton—an African American working-class community; Roadville—a white working-class community; and a mainstream Piedmont Carolinas community made up of both whites and African Americans. Over the time period of almost 10 years, Heath observed spontaneous parent-child interactions, took field notes, and made tape-recordings. Mothers in the mainstream homes also made their own tape-recordings.

Results ❖ Verbal interaction with parents emerged as an outstanding predictor of success in school. Heath found that in Trackton, parents did not see preschoolers as appropriate conversation partners. Roadville parents engaged in talk with their preschoolers more frequently than Trackton parents did. Mainstream parents engaged their children in sustained talk far more often than both Trackton and Roadville parents. They were also the only ones who tended to prepare children for school and then reinforce school behavior and learning at home. Both Trackton and Roadville children did not maintain a pattern of success in school, while mainstream children, with few exceptions, did.

Implications for Teaching ❖ The importance of parent-child verbal interaction and parental involvement in the education process must be communicated to parents of preschoolers. Teachers need to be aware that children enter school with varying degrees of advantage or disadvantage produced by lack or presence of parental verbal interaction and involvement and address such needs in every way possible.

Heath, S.B., & Thomas, C. (1984). The achievement of preschool literacy for mother and child. In H. Goelman, A.A. Oberg, & F. Smith (Eds.), *Awakening to Literacy* (pp. 51–72). Portsmouth, NH: Heinemann.

Purpose of the Study ❖ To discover what associated behaviors and adjustments of verbal and nonverbal behavior accompany book reading with a preschooler.

Procedures ❖ Over the period of a year, Heath introduced literacy artifacts with minimal guidance to her subjects, a 16-year-old African

American mother and her 2-year-old son, and observed the verbal interactions and literacy activities that took place between them. (They were residents of the Trackton community in the Piedmont Carolinas.) Heath used her own field notes as well as the mother's written observations and audio-tapes.

Results ❖ The introduction of book reading in this household provided new ways for the adults to speak to the child and changed their perceptions about caregivers' and children's roles. There was also an increased awareness of the child's language development and new patterns of talking about language.

Implications for Teaching ❖ Heath's model of parent as researcher indicates that teachers can benefit greatly from parental input and involvement and should use parents as a resource rather than assume that parents, especially those with limited education, are unable to help.

Jacob, E. (1984). *Learning literacy through play: Puerto Rican kindergarten children.* In H. Goelman, A.A. Oberg, & F. Smith (Eds.), *Awakening to literacy* (pp. 73–83). Portsmouth, NH: Heinemann.

Purpose of the Study ❖ To examine the literacy activities of children during play and the role of these activities in their learning of social behaviors and skills associated with literacy.

Procedures ❖ Jacobs and four assistants observed a random sample (stratified by sex) of 29 children aged 5 to 6 in Utuado, Puerto Rico. There were 10 middle-class boys, 4 middle-class girls, 8 lower-class girls, and 7 lower-class boys. The observers used field notes and tape-recordings. Four home observations per child were conducted, two lasting 15 minutes and two lasting 30 minutes. Each of the children's primary female caregivers was interviewed twice, before the observations began and after they were completed.

Results ❖ Forty-eight percent of the children engaged in literacy skill activities during play, producing 25 of about 50 possible types of literacy skill activities in the areas of counting, reading, and writing (in this descending order of frequency). Girls performed more literacy activities than boys, and only girls acted out social roles associated with literacy during play.

Implications for Teaching ❖ Teachers can create opportunities for literacy learning in the context of play and can plan play events and materials accordingly.

Lynch, E.C., Blaska, J.K., & Crawford, L.W. (1994). Intergenerational literacy practices in rural midwestern families. [Funded by the U.S. Office of Education and Moorhead State University]

Purpose of the Study ❖ This study addressed components of intergenerational transmission of literacy routines in three groups of rural, midwestern families: (1) mothers of children who were enrolled in a public-school, community-based interagency early intervention program for young children with identified disabilities, (2) mothers of young children who were enrolled in a community childcare program operated by a regional state university, and (3) mothers of children enrolled in the local Head Start program.

Procedures ❖ Data were collected in triangulated fashion using: life history interviews, home and classroom literacy checklists, and an extensive questionnaire on reading and writing practices completed by family members and analyzed for themes and patterns within and across groups. Case studies of individual families are being developed.

Results ❖ The data indicated that literacy events such as reading to their child, writing with their child, and encouraging their child's interest in print were integral parts of their family rituals and routines regardless of income level or presence or absence of disability.

Implications for Teaching ❖ Rural midwestern parents are creating literacy environments and experiences that build on their past and incorporate the present, and schools need to affirm these parental efforts in providing family literacy environments and experiences. The study supports beliefs about the importance and influence of intergenerational transmission of literacy that are a part of a family's culture, and teachers must recognize the value of these rituals and routines.

Madigan, D. (1992). Family uses of literacy: A critical voice. In C.K. Kinzer, et al. (Eds.), *Literacy research, theory, and practice: Views from many perspectives* (pp. 87–99). Chicago, IL: National Reading Conference, Inc.

Purpose of the Study ❖ To provide insight into the value and function of literacy in the lives of three adults who valued writing as an important means of self-expression in spite of life circumstances that were contrary to the development of a literate identity.

Procedures ❖ Madigan relied on methods of naturalistic inquiry. Over the period of a year, he held bi-weekly visits in which he recorded interviews and collected written artifacts from three African American adults in a large Midwestern urban community.

Results ❖ All three participants grew up in a home, school, or social environment that was hostile to their efforts as writers. Nonetheless, each continued to value the meaning of literacy and self-expression and continued to make writing an important part of their lives in spite of obstacles.

Implications for Teaching ❖ At all grade levels, teachers must respect and encourage literacy efforts and the risk-taking involved in the writing process. Parents should also be educated about the importance of not hurting their child's self-esteem by rejecting literacy efforts instead of encouraging the child in a constructive way.

Ortiz, V. (1986). Reading activities and reading proficiency among Hispanic, black, and white students. *American Journal of Education* (November 1986), 58–76.

Purpose of the Study ❖ To examine the extent to which lower reading proficiency among Hispanic and black children is explained by parents' educational level and by reading activities in the home and to examine the direct effects of parents' education and reading activities among minority and nonminority children.

Procedures ❖ Analysis of the National Assessment of Education Progress's survey of reading proficiency among in-school fourth, eighth, and eleventh graders was used.

Results ❖ No one factor explained a large portion of the differences among racial and ethnic groups. Parents' reading activities were found to directly affect the reading proficiency of both minority and nonminority children.

Implications for Teaching ❖ Parents should be made aware of their importance as reading role models, regardless of their educational levels or socioeconomic backgrounds.

Purcell-Gates, V. (1994). Relationships between parental literacy skills and functional uses of print and children's ability to learn literacy skills. National Institute for Literacy (Grant #X257A20223): Washington, D.C.

Purpose of the Study ❖ To examine the relationships between what young children learn about written language in the home and their parents' levels of literacy ability and their everyday uses of print.

Procedures ❖ Twenty-four children between the ages of 4 and 6 in 20 families of low socioeconomic status were observed during their waking hours in their homes and communities for an aggregated week. Researchers, assuming participant observer roles, noted all instances of uses of print within the homes and families. They also administered a series of tasks to the focal children, designed to measure critical written language concepts found to influence the degree of success young children experience in beginning literacy instruction.

Results ❖ Overall, a low level of print use was found in the homes, although variation did exist. Families tended to use print mainly for entertainment purposes and daily living routines. The greatest proportion of text used in the homes was at the clausal/phrasal level, such as food coupons and container print. The next most used level was at the full written discourse level of complexity found in books, magazines, and documents. The children as a group displayed a below-average knowledge of written language concepts. Children whose parents read and write on their own at more complex levels of text *and* who read and write *with their children* begin formal literacy instruction knowing more about critical written language concepts than those children whose parents do not. Parents with lower levels of literacy do less of this and thus are unable to help their children acquire the concepts in the home that will be needed to make sense of instruction in school. Results also showed that schooling made a big difference regarding the acquisition of this knowledge for these children. Further, adult education programs that focus on *family literacy* positively influence both the frequency of literacy events and of mother/child interaction around literacy.

Implications for Teaching ❖ Teachers must ascertain the degree to which their beginning readers and writers possess critical written language skills and adapt instruction accordingly. They also need to facilitate home literacy by working with the parents and providing materials and activity suggestions. Family literacy programs that help parents learn to incorporate literacy into home activities and to elicit and respond to children's questions about print should be encouraged.

Schlieffelin, B.B., & Cochran-Smith, M. (1984). Learning to read culturally: Literacy before schooling. In H. Goelman, A.A. Oberg, & F. Smith (Eds.), *Awakening to literacy* (pp. 3–23). Portsmouth, NH: Heinemann.

Purpose of the Study ❖ To find and compare recurrent cultural patterns of early literacy acquisition in three diverse social groups.

Procedures ❖ Three social groups were studied: (1) educated, school-oriented parents and their preschoolers in a Philadelphia, PA, suburb; (2) a family in the traditionally non-literate Kaluli society in Papua, New Guinea; and (3) a number of Chinese families who left Vietnam and settled in Philadelphia. Audio-recordings of story-reading events, formal interviews, and field notes were used.

Results ❖ Without exception, families in the first group (Philadelphia, well-educated) read stories to their children frequently and regularly. Literacy in the Kaluli society was introduced by Christian missionaries in 1971 to promote reading of the Bible. In the Kaluli community, literacy was seen as an element that separated individuals in society and was not seen as a relevant or necessary part of the lives of most people. In the Sino-Vietnamese group, home literacy activities were conducted mostly in Chinese and consisted primarily of letter writing and reading. The acquisition of functional literacy in English was a priority of this group. The researchers conclude that in order for an individual to become literate, literacy must be functional, relevant, and meaningful in the context of his or her society.

Implications for Teaching ❖ Awareness that literacy comes in many forms, including oral history, in various ethnic traditions should promote an open-minded approach to introducing literacy and encouraging its reinforcement in the home.

Taylor, D. (1983). *Family literacy: Young children learning to read and write.* Portsmouth, NH: Heinemann.

Purpose of the Study ❖ To "develop systematic ways of looking at reading and writing as activities that have consequences in and are affected by family life."

Procedures ❖ Six families with a total of 15 children who were all between the ages of 2 and 17 were studied for 16 months. The families had varied socioeconomic and educational levels and represented diverse racial and ethnic backgrounds. Interviews, field notes, and audio-tapes were used. Parents' memories of literacy experiences and how these carried over to their current families were studied, as was children's awareness of written language at home, school, and in various social situations.

Results ❖ Taylor concluded that "literacy develops best in relational contexts which are meaningful to the young child." Literacy needs to be relevant to a child's experiences. Community-based literacy programs should be designed in part by the participants themselves. If literacy becomes socially significant in the life of the parent, it will be likely to be significant in the life of the child.

Implications for Teaching ❖ It is vital to relate reading and writing to the everyday experiences with which students are able to identify in order to render literacy meaningful. Presenting literacy in social contexts will also contribute to its importance and meaning.

Taylor, D. (1986). Creating family story: "Matthew, we're going to have a ride!" In W.H. Teale & E. Sulzby (Eds.), *Emergent literacy: Writing and reading* (pp. 139–155). Norwood, NJ: Ablex.

Purpose of the Study ❖ To discover "new ways of developing natural histories of family literacy."

Procedures ❖ Taylor developed a text from listening to the audio-tape of a family story-reading event.

Results ❖ Taylor reflects that the patterns of family literacy events develop literacy skills and enable children to construct social and environmental relationships. To gain insight into the significance of storybook reading events, Taylor offers questions for further study.

Implications for Teaching ❖ By balancing knowledge of language and literacy development with an understanding of social and cultural family circumstances, teachers can learn more about the ways in which children gain access to "the social world of their literate heritage" and find new and exciting ways to encourage family involvement in literacy.

Taylor, D., & Dorsey-Gaines, C. (1988). *Growing up literate: Learning from inner-city families.* Portsmouth, NH: Heinemann.

Purpose of the Study ❖ To examine children's development of literacy in the context of home and family.

Procedures ❖ The subjects of this study were four African American families living in the same inner-city neighborhood, who had children in the first grade who were successfully learning to read and write. Field notes and other ethnographic methods of study were used. A detailed account of the families' daily lives and the function of literacy in these homes is provided.

Results ❖ The researchers concluded that socioeconomic status and educational attainment cannot necessarily be considered predictors of literacy attainment. All of the families studied created opportunities for their children to learn. Their homes were filled with functional print and the children lived in structured homes where literacy was learned through social interactions and various literacy activities.

Implications for Teaching ❖ Teachers need to be aware that literacy opportunities can be created in all types of homes and on all socio-economic and educational levels. The "deficit model" is not the best approach. Parents' efforts at involvement should be welcomed and encouraged in a culturally appropriate way.

Teale, W.H. (1986). Home background and young children's literacy development. In W.H. Teale & E. Sulzby (Eds.), *Emergent literacy: Writing and reading* (pp. 173–203). Norwood, NJ: Ablex.

Purpose of the Study ❖ To explore the relation between home background and young children's literacy development.

Procedures ❖ Systematic observations were made of 24 preschool children from low-income families of various ethnic backgrounds over a period of 3 to 18 months. Equal numbers of boys and girls between the ages of 2 1/2 and 3 1/2 were studied. Field notes and audio-tapes were used during the home observations, which totaled 1,400 hours.

Results ❖ A variety of reading materials was available in all the homes. However, a common problem was locating paper and writing materials when children requested them. Only in three homes were writing implements stored in a special place, and it was in these homes that the participant children who did the most writing lived. In the other homes, by the time this material was located, children often lost their interest in using paper and pen/pencils. The most striking feature of literacy observed was its social nature.

Implications for Teaching ❖ Teachers should make parents aware that the simple, inexpensive practice of storing writing materials in one specific place can have an impact on their children's emergent literacy practices. The social component of literacy should also be incorporated into classroom activities.

Tracey, D. (1994). *Mother-child interactions during children's oral reading at home.* Unpublished doctoral dissertation, Rutgers University, New Brunswick, NJ.

Purpose of the Study ❖ The purpose of this investigation was to study the ways in which mothers help their children during children's oral reading at home. Specifically, the conversations of 26 accelerated 3rd grade readers and their college-educated mothers were compared with the conversations of 26 at-risk 3rd grade readers and their college-educated mothers.

Procedures ❖ Each child read two sets of reading materials at home to his/her mother; one set of material was at the child's individual instructional level of difficulty and the other was at the child's grade level. Audiotapes were professionally transcribed and then coded according to four major categories of interaction: (1) error correction strategies used by mothers, (2) questioning strategies used by mothers, (3) commenting strategies used by mothers, and (4) total words spoken by the child. The data were analyzed using an analysis of variance with reading ability, sex, and text difficulty (repeated measure) as the independent measures and the coding interactions described above as the dependent measures.

Results ❖ The results of the analysis yielded significant differences in the areas of background data, effects of reading ability, and effects of text difficulty. No significant main effects related to sex were identified. Specifically, the analysis revealed that at-risk readers practiced significantly more at-home oral reading at the 2nd and 3rd grade levels than did their accelerated peers; however, significant differences were not found at the first grade level. Both groups of readers were significantly affected by the difficulty of the text they read, with harder texts associated with greater parent/child interactions of all types. When performances of the two groups were compared on instructional level materials, mothers of accelerated readers used more support stategies during reading than did mothers of at-risk readers. When performances of the two groups were compared on grade level materials, mothers of at-risk readers used more error correction interventions than did mothers of accelerated readers.

Implications for Teaching ❖ Educators should consider refining their recommendations with regard to having children practice reading at home. While reading easier text has traditionally been recommended for at-risk readers in an effort to build their reading fluency, the present investigation suggests that the use of harder text promotes mother-child discussion and conversation during reading. Additionally, teachers may want to help parents of at-risk readers develop greater use of reading support strategies, such as asking high level questions and relating text concepts to their children's lives.

Wagner, D.A., & Spratt, J.E. (1988). Intergenerational literacy: Effects of parental literacy and attitudes on children's reading achievement in Morocco. *Human Development, 31,* 359–369.

Purpose of the Study ❖ To investigate the specific role of parental literacy and attitudes on children's literacy acquisition.

Procedures ❖ This 5-year longitudinal study involved a sample of 350 6- to 7-year-old Moroccan children and their parents. Data reported includes a sociodemocratic and attitudinal survey. Parents were questioned on their beliefs about reading habits, development, and self-perception within the context of their children's academic and literacy development. Tests were given to the children to assess reading abilities and metacognitive beliefs about reading behavior and attitudes.

Results ❖ Although in many cases, parental educational levels seemed more relevant to a child's development than socioeconomic status, a full third of the highest scoring readers had parents who had never attended school. Certain clusters of beliefs and attitudes in parents strongly predicted children's metacognitive beliefs about reading achievement.

Implications for Teaching ❖ Teachers should take every opportunity to enhance parental attitudes toward literacy in its many forms regardless of the parent's educational or socioeconomic background.

Agencies and Associations that Deal with Family Literacy

❖ **American Library Association**
Bell Atlantic ALA Family Literacy Project
50 East Huron St.
Chicago, IL 60611

> This project encourages libraries to develop and improve library-based family literacy projects for ethnic minorities and the rural and urban poor. Fact sheets on family literacy and how to start a project as well as information on contact persons are provided.

❖ **The Barbara Bush Foundation for Family Literacy**
1002 Wisconsin Avenue NW
Washington, DC 20007

> The Barbara Bush Foundation for Family Literacy is an all-volunteer endeavor established in 1989. Its mission

is to support the development of family literacy programs, to break the intergenerational cycle of illiteracy, and to establish literacy as a value in every American family. The foundation identifies successful family literacy efforts; awards grants to help establish family literacy programs; provides seed money for community planning of inter-agency programs; supports training and professional development for teachers; encourages recognition of volunteers, educators, students, and effective programs; and publishes and distributes materials that document effective working programs. The foundation also provides speakers. Grants totaling $500,000 have been awarded annually since 1990 to build family literacy programs throughout the country.

❖ Children's Television Workshop (CTW)
One Lincoln Plaza
New York, NY 10023

Children's Television Workshop (CTW) serves children, families, and care-givers in a variety of settings, including homes, preschools, before- and after-school settings, and during leisure time. CTW produces the Sesame Street Pre-School Education Program (PEP), which is designed to enhance early childhood learning. Ghostwriter is CTW's multimedia project for 7- to 10-year-old children, designed to promote reading and writing activities. Included are a weekly television series, free monthly magazines, a weekly newspaper page, and books (from Bantam). CTW also publishes a number of magazines at various reading levels with highly motivating visuals. All contain features that can be enjoyed by more than one family member.

❖ Correctional Education Association (CEA)
8025 Laurel Lakes Court
Laurel, MI 20702

The Correctional Education Association (CEA) serves incarcerated adults and juveniles in prisons, jails, juvenile facilities, and community corrections. CEA runs some basic programs with inmates trained as tutors. The **Motheread** program, which is offered in two North Carolina prisons, is the family literacy effort in which CEA participates.

❖ Even Start Program
Compensatory Education Programs
400 Maryland Avenue, SW
Room 2043
Washington, DC 20202

The Even Start Program (of the U.S. Department of Education) funds family-centered education projects designed to help parents become partners in the education of their children while improving their own literacy skills. Local school districts in all states may apply for funds.

❖ Family English Literacy Programs
Office of Bilingual Education and Minority Language Affairs
400 Maryland Avenue, SW, Room 5620
Washington, DC 20202

This U.S. Department of Education program offers funds to help adults with limited English language proficiency achieve competence in the language and provides information on how parents and family members can promote the educational development of children. Local school districts, colleges, universities, and private non-profit groups are eligible for assistance.

❖ Harvard Family Research Project

Longfellow Hall
Harvard Graduate School of Education
Appian Way
Cambridge, MA 02138

The Harvard Family Research Project conducts research into educational programs that enhance child, adult, and family development. The project disseminates information about state and family support and education initiatives and policies, about the effectiveness of these programs, and about the development of programs in various public and private agencies. A national resource guide to public-school affiliated programs is available.

❖ Head Start Bureau

P.O. Box 1182
Washington, DC 20013

Administered by the Department of Health and Human Services, the Head Start Program has provided comprehensive child-development services to low-income families for 25 years. Since 1984, a special emphasis has been placed on promoting literacy and basic education for the parents and children in the program. Head Start joined forces with Literacy Volunteers of America (LVA) in 1988 to create a family literacy program in which LVA-trained tutors offer one-on-one instruction to parents of Head Start children at 24 sites in New York and New

Jersey. Local Head Start programs coordinate such services as transportation to facilitate literacy training.

❖ International Reading Association (IRA)

800 Barksdale Road
P.O. Box 8139
Newark, DE 19714-8139

The International Reading Association (IRA) serves teachers, librarians, administrators, and reading specialists. The mission of the IRA Family Literacy Commission is to explore the types of family literacy programs that are in existence and to disseminate to its constituency information on what is available. The commission does so through conference presentations and publications. The work of the educators includes presentations about family literacy at IRA conferences and in journal articles, themed issues of journals, books, and monographs. The IRA's purpose is to describe existing programs, not to develop them, and to let the public know what is good practice. The IRA provides a broad perspective on family literacy and is willing to offer expertise to other organizations.

❖ Laubach Literacy Action (LLA)

1320 Jamesville Avenue
Box 131
Syracuse, NY 13210

The Laubach Literacy Action (LLA) serves adult learners, literacy volunteers, trainers, program administrators, and board members. The LLA is the U.S. branch of Laubach Literacy International (LLI), a nonprofit educational corporation that manages a worldwide network of literacy programs. The purpose of LLA is to enable adults within the United States to acquire basic level skills in listening, speaking, reading, writing, and mathematics. New Readers Press, the publishing division of Laubach Literacy International, publishes material for use in family literacy programs. A recent publication is *Family Literacy in Action,* which spotlights several successful family literacy programs throughout the country.

❖ Library Literacy Program
Office of Library Programs
555 New Jersey Avenue, NW, Suite 400
Washington, DC 20208

This U.S. Department of Education program provides grants to state and local public libraries to support literacy programs. A variety of approaches to family literacy is represented in some of the library literacy projects that have been funded. Both state and local libraries may apply for funds.

❖ Literacy Volunteers of America, Inc. (LVA)
Southeast Regional Office
5455 N. McDonough Street
Suite C
Decatur, GA 30030

Literacy Volunteers of America (LVA) is a national, nonprofit, educational organization founded in 1962 to combat the problem of adult illiteracy in the United States. Today LVA has more than 450 affiliate programs nationwide. LVA provides materials and services to assist in the development of volunteer tutorial programs in basic literacy and English as a second language for adults throughout the United States and Canada. In 1990, LVA became involved in launching a program to teach parents and caregivers with low literacy skills how to read to their children.

❖ National Coalition of Title 1/Chapter 1 Parents
Edmonds School Building
9th and D Streets, NE, Second Floor
Washington, DC 20002

This organization was established in 1973 by 50 parents to help other parents become actively involved in their children's education. The Coalition sponsors a yearly National In-Service Training Conference which brings together parents, educators, administrators, and community representatives to exchange information on ways to maximize education. A bimonthly newsletter, on-site technical assistance workshops, and a student financial assistance award are also provided.

❖ National Center for Family Literacy (NCFL)
401 South 4th Avenue
Suite 610
Louisville, KY 40202-3449

The National Center for Family Literacy (NCFL) is a private, nonprofit corporation developed with a grant from the William R. Kenan, Jr., Charitable Trust, that was established for the purpose of expanding the efforts to solve the problem of illiteracy through family literacy programs. NCFL consists of a cadre of experts specializing in education and family intervention techniques, who provide extensive training and technical assistance to enable quality family literacy programs to be established nationwide. NCFL encourages a national understanding and response to the problem of intergenerational low-educational achievement through assistance and information provided to federal, state, and local policy makers and program planners; funds and assists the establishment of family literacy model programs; conducts research to improve the quality of family literacy efforts; and supports the expansion of family literacy programs nationwide. The NCFL also serves as a national clearinghouse for information and develops new materials, disseminating information on current practice.

❖ National PTA

700 N. Rush Street
Chicago, IL 60611-2571

The National PTA supports state and local PTA units. Each local unit has the authorization to implement a family literacy project if it so chooses. The National PTA encourages the formation of coalitions with other groups to implement programs that will break the intergenerational cycle of illiteracy.

❖ Push Literacy Action Now, Inc. (PLAN)

1332 G Street, SE
Washington, DC 20003

PLAN is a private, nonprofit voluntary adult literacy program that publishes *The Ladder*, a national literacy newsletter. PLAN offers special literacy training for parents through its community-oriented literacy training and advocacy program. PLAN developed a family literacy model called Take Up Reading Now (TURN) and provides a family literacy kit, *Laying the Foundations*, which includes guidelines for creating a parent-child curriculum and resource materials for literacy tutors.

❖ Reading Is Fundamental, Inc. (RIF)
5500 Maryland Avenue, SW
Washington, DC 20024

Reading Is Fundamental (RIF) primarily serves young people from infancy through high school in diverse settings: schools, libraries, day-care centers, community centers, hospitals, public housing, prisons, migrant labor camps, and Indian reservations. RIF's mission is to encourage and support children in their efforts to become strong, committed readers. RIF involves parents and other family members in all of its programs and also provides free books. RIF offers programs that are designed to guide and support parents in their efforts to make family literacy a priority. RIF's motivational and activity-based approach is designed to complement direct instructional approaches. In addition to its many programs, RIF offers publications and technical assistance via staff and program materials.

❖ Rural Clearinghouse for Lifelong Education and Development
111 College Court
Kansas State University
Manhattan, KS 66506

The Rural Clearinghouse serves educational providers at colleges and universities, community colleges, cooperative extensions, and libraries that are working to expand educational opportunities to rural learners. The Rural Clearinghouse is a national effort to improve rural access to education. Its work includes disseminating effective models for serving rural areas; facilitating the development of effective educational models in response to selected rural problems; providing forums for the exchange of information among education professionals; developing regionally organized and supported networks; and advocating rural needs with educational associations and state and federal policy makers. The Rural Clearinghouse's book, *Literacy in Rural America,* is a study that offers a look at how rural centers incorporate literacy into family initiatives.

❖ UNICEF
3 United Nations Plaza
New York, NY 10017

UNICEF serves children, youth, and adults in developing countries worldwide. At the headquarters level, UNICEF includes family literacy in concept/policy efforts within the field of literacy. At the country level, there are several UNICEF offices that are supporting family literacy projects. UNICEF offices throughout the world offer resources on the family literacy effort.

❖ U.S. Department of Education
Clearinghouse on Adult Education
U.S. Department of Education
Division of Adult Education
Mary E. Switzer Building
400 Maryland Avenue, SW
Washington, DC 20201

This clearinghouse offers free information on family literacy. Publications available include descriptions of family literacy programs, fact sheets, and bibliographies.

Further References about Family Literacy

Books

Boehnlein, M., & Hager, B. (1985). *Children, parents, and reading: An annotated bibliography.* Newark, DE: International Reading Association.

Delgado-Gaitan, C. (1990). *Literacy for empowerment: The role of parents in children's education.* New York: The Falmer Press.

Lareau, A. (1990). *Home advantage.* New York: The Falmer Press.

Moll, L.C. (1992). Literacy research in community and classrooms: A sociocultural approach. In R. Beach, J. Green, M.L. Kamil, & T. Shanahan (Eds.), *Multidisciplinary perspectives on literacy research,* (pp. 211–244). Urbana, IL: NCRE and CCTE.

Morrow, L.M. (1995). *Family literacy connections in schools and communities.* Newark, DE: International Reading Association.

Morrow, L.M. (1993). *Literacy development in the early years: Helping children read and write.* Boston, MA: Allyn & Bacon.

Roser, N. (1989). *Helping your child become a better reader.* Newark, DE: International Reading Association.

Silberman, A. (1989). *Growing up writing.* New York: Random House.

Smith, P. (1986). *Parents and teacher together.* London, England: McMillan Education, Ltd.

Strickland, D., & Taylor, D. (1986). *Family storybook reading.* Portsmouth, NH: Heinemann.

Articles

Auerbach, E.R. (1990). Making meaning, making change. A guide to participatory curriculum development for adult ESL and family literacy. Boston, MA: University of Massuchusetts, English Family Literacy Project.

Carlson, C.G. (1991). Getting parents involved in their children's education. *The Education Digest, 57*(3), 10–12.

Cohen, D.L. (1992). Aiming for literacy across two generations, Even Start teaches a parent to teach a child. *Education Week, 11*(31).

Daisey, P. (1991). Intergenerational literacy programs: Rationale, description, and effectiveness. *Journal of Clinical Child Psychology, 20,* 11–17.

Darling, S. (1988). *Family literacy: Replacing the cycle of failure with the legacy of success. Evaluation report of the Kenan Trust Family Literacy Project.* Louisville, KY. (ERIC Document Reproduction Service No. ED 332 794)

Dornbusch, S.G., Ritter P.L. (1988). Parents of high school students: A neglected resource. *Educational Horizons, 66*(2), 75–77.

Epstein, J. (1988). How do we improve programs for parental involvement? *Educational Horizons, 66,* 55–59.

Even Start. (1990). *Program Abstracts.* Washington, DC: Office of Vocational and Adult Education. (ERIC Document Reproduction Service No. ED 339 484)

Family reading is goal of New PBA series. (1989). *Reading Today, 7*(2), 28.

Fredericks, A.D., & Taylor, D. (1985). *Parent programs in reading: Guidelines for success.* Newark, DE: International Reading Association.

Gadsden, V.L. (1992). Giving meaning to literacy: Intergenerational beliefs about access. *Theory into Practice, 31,* 328–336.

Glover, R.J., et al. (1991a). Family literacy: A formative evaluation of program outcomes. *Contemporary Education, 62*(1), 324–326.

Glover, R.J., et al. (1991b). Promoting family literacy: An alternative intervention. *Journal of Instructional Psychology, 18,* 194–204.

Handel, R.D., & Goldsmith, E. (1988). Intergenerational literacy: A community college program. *Journal of Reading, 32*(3).

Hannon, P. (1987). A study of the effects of parental involvement in the teaching of reading on children's reading test performance. *British Journal of Educational Psychology, 57,* 56–72.

Hannon, P., Jackson, A., & Weinberger, J. (1986). Parents' and teachers' strategies in hearing young children read. *Research Papers in Education, 1*, 6–25.

Johnson, D.W., & Edmonds, M.L. (1990). *Family literacy: Models of service.* Iowa State Library, Des Moines. (ERIC Document Reproduction Service No. ED 328 269)

Jongsma, K.S. (1990). Intergenerational literacy. *The Reading Teacher, 43*, 522–523.

Lancey, D.F., Draper, K.D., & Boyce, F. (1989). Parental influence on children's acquisition of reading. *Contemporary Issues in Reading, 4*(1), 83–93.

Monaghan, J. (1991). Family literacy in early 18th century Boston, MA: Cotton Mather and his children. *Reading Research Quarterly, 26*(4), 342–370.

NFO Research, Inc. (1990). *Reading Rainbow Study. Final Report.* (ERIC Document Reproduction Service No. ED 331 027)

Nickse, R.S. (1990a). *Family and intergenerational literacy programs: An update of "The Noises of Literacy."* Washington, DC: Office of Educational Research and Development. (ERIC Document Reproduction Service No. ED 327 736)

Nickse, R.S. (1990b). Family literacy programs: Ideas for action. *Adult Learning, 1*, 9–13.

Nickse, R.S. (1991). *A typology of family and intergenerational literacy programs: Implications for evaluation.* Paper presented at the annual meeting of the American Educational Research Association, Chicago, IL. (ERIC Document Reproduction Service No. ED 333 166)

Nuckolls, M.E. (1991). Expanding students' potential through family literacy. *Education Leadership, 49*, 45–46.

Padak, N., & Cook, D. (1990). *Family literacy programs training manual.* Columbus, OH: Ohio State Department of Education, Division of Adult Basic Education. (ERIC Document Reproduction Service No. ED 329 731)

Paratore, J. (1994). Parents and children sharing literacy. In D. Lancy (Ed.), *Emergent literacy: From research to practice.* New York: Praeger.

Paratore, J. (1992). *An intergenerational approach to literacy: Effects on the literacy learning of adults and on the practice of family literacy.* Paper presented at the annual meeting of the National Reading Conference, San Antonio, TX.

Parker, M.J. (1989). Building bridges in midtown Manhattan: An intergenerational literacy program. *Urban Education, 24*(1).

Pellingrini, A.D., et al. (1991). Joint reading between black Head Start children and their mothers. *Child Development, 61,* 443–453.

Quintero, E., & Velarde, M.C. (1990). Intergenerational literacy: A developmental bilingual approach. *Young children, 45,* 10–15.

Radecki, K.K. (1987). *An annotated bibliography of the literature examining the importance of adults reading aloud to children.* Washington, DC: U.S. Department of Education. (ERIC Document Reproduction Service No. ED 294 274)

Roscow, L.V. (1991). How schools perpetuate illiteracy. *Education Leadership, 49,* 41–44.

Ryan, K.E., et al. (1991). *An evaluation framework for family literacy programs.* Paper presented at the annual meeting of the American Educational Research Association, Chicago, IL. (ERIC Document Reproduction Service No. ED 331 029)

Seaman, D., et al. (1991). *Follow-up study of the impact of the Keenan Trust Model for Family Literacy.* Louisville, KY: National Center for Family Literacy. (ERIC Document Reproduction Service No. ED 340 479)

Segal, E., & Friedberg, J.B. (1991a). Is today liberry day? Community support for family literacy. *Language Arts, 68,* 654–657.

Segal, E., & Friedberg, J.B. (1991b). Widening the circle: The Beginning with Books Model. *The Horn Book Magazine, 67,* 186–189.

Smith, Carl B. (1991). Parents sharing books. *Annual Report 1990–1991.* Bloomington, IN: Family Literacy Center, Indiana University. (ERIC Document Reproduction Service No. ED 335 645)

Stiles, R.E. (1991). *Family literacy: An annotated bibliography and selected public library program descriptions.* (Unpublished master's thesis, University of North Carolina, Chapel Hill). (ERIC Document Reproduction Service No. ED 332 731)

Strickland, D.S., & Morrow, L.M. (1990). Emerging readers & writers: Family literacy: Sharing good books. *Reading Teacher, 43*(7), 518–519.

Sway, S.M. (1987). *Enhancing parent involvement in schools.* New York: Teachers College Press.

Wagner, D.A., & Spratt, J. (1988). Intergenerational literacy: Effects of parental literacy and attitudes on children's reading achievement in Morocco. *Human Development, 31,* 359–369.

Weinstein-Shr, G. (1990). *Family and intergenerational literacy in multilingual families.* National Clearinghouse on Literacy Education: An Adjunct of ERIC Clearinghouse.

Wilks, F.T.J., & Clark, V.A. (1988). Training versus nontraining of mothers as home reading tutors. *Perceptual and Motor Skills,* 67, 135–142.

Winter, M., & Rouse, J. (1990). Fostering intergenerational literacy: The Missouri Parents as Teachers Program. *The Reading Teacher,* 43(6).

Index of Family
Literacy Programs

This monograph is sponsored by the Family Literacy Commission of the International Reading Association. The Commission is charged with conducting research and creating professional materials in the area of family literacy.